CREATION AT WORSHIP

CREATION AT WORSHIP

Christopher J. Voke

Paternoster:
thinking faith

MILTON KEYNES ● COLORADO SPRINGS ● HYDERABAD

First published 2009 by Paternoster
Paternoster is an imprint of Authentic Media
9 Holdom Avenue, Bletchley, Milton Keynes, Bucks, MK1 1QR, UK
1820 Jet Stream Drive, Colorado Springs, CO 80921, USA
OM Authentic Media, Medchal Road, Jeedimetla Village,
Secunderabad 500 055, A.P., India
www.authenticmedia.co.uk

Authentic Media is a division of IBS-STL U.K., limited by guarantee, with its
Registered Office at Kingstown Broadway, Carlisle, Cumbria CA3 0HA.
Registered in England & Wales No. 1216232. Registered charity 270162

British Library Cataloguing in Publication Data
A catalogue record for this book is available from the
British Library
ISBN-13: 978-1-84227-645-7

Cover design by fourninezero design
Print Management by Adare
Printed and bound in Great Britain by J F Print Ltd., Sparkford, Somerset

Contents

Preface

This book has been written with ministers and students in mind, reflecting my own present role in the teaching and formation of those who are preparing for Christian ministry or leadership. They are people who will be ultimately responsible for public worship in the churches. But there are also many others in church life who have influence, and these are not only those at the front with speaking or singing parts. Christian believers feel deeply about the worship of their church, many think deeply about it, and their voices are part of this conversation. It is to those who make the decisions, those who care and those who have a view about what goes on in worship services, that the message of this book is offered.

It has been a labour of love in three dimensions. Like many who live in the small and crowded United Kingdom, I have always been at home in the British countryside. God's natural world is always in my mind. Having lived most of the time in cities the natural creation acts in my life as a place of restoration, retreat and revelation. Its ecological abuse is a cause of sadness and its neglect a source of anger. Then also I am an advocate of public worship; a singer, a musician and an eager responder to well-ordered and inspiring worship. I hope therefore, in some small way, that the argument being made here will influence Christian public worship to be richer, more pleasing to the God we serve and more beneficial to us all. Then, finally, I have always instinctively sought breadth and balance, the longer and broader view of God's activity, and I have therefore looked for the widest brackets to incorporate Christian theology; the holiness with the friendship of God, his dramatic revelation by the prophet's word and his voice in the godly wisdom of human experience, his work in saving deliverance and his presence in sustaining blessing. The truth in Christian thinking is found in extremes, but extremities held together boldly and with final submission to the mystery. This breadth of view has motivated me to hope and work for the church at worship deliberately reaching out in declaring the saving acts of God while grasping also the dimension of his creating work.

It is right to acknowledge colleagues, research supervisors and students who have influenced the thinking behind this book. My immediate colleagues at Spurgeon's College have been the most obvious source of inspiration and challenge. In particular I want to mention my former colleague and Old Testament scholar, the late Martin Selman, who for me, as for others I suspect, opened new doors both in thinking and in life-opportunity. My family too have borne much in the long preparation and production of this book, particularly my wife Margaret to whom I am for ever grateful.

Chris Voke, Spurgeon's College, Spring 2009

Abbreviations

ANF	*The Ante-Nicene Fathers*
BCP	*The Book of Common Prayer*
Cat.	*Catechism of the Catholic Church*
CD	Barth's *Church Dogmatics*
CW	*Common Worship: Services and Prayers for the Church of England*
DL	*The Divine Liturgy of our father among the saints John Chrysostom*
Inst.	Calvin's *Institutes of the Christian Religion*
LW	*Luther's Works*
MM	*A Manual for Ministers*
Miss.	*The Missal in Latin and English*
MWB	*The Methodist Worship Book*
OP	*Orders and Prayers for Church Worship*
PP	*Patterns and Prayers for Christian Worship*
SMiss.	*The Sunday Missal*

1

Setting the Scene

Teach us as children to speak to the Father,
and yet as creatures to bow before our Maker.

(*C.H. Spurgeon*)[1]

Going into a local church for Sunday worship in the twenty-first century is a mixed experience. You may be delighted or horrified and, unless you know the particular church well, there is no telling which it will be. Such a visit, however, is rarely without interest since you can never be sure exactly what is going to happen. There are so many possibilities. You may be caught up into a vibrant informal contemporary musical extravaganza, or drawn into a meditative and carefully led collection of ancient and contemporary liturgy. Or you may find yourself in a kind of time warp, in a service that is the same as those you attended many years ago.

Nor is this variety of content dependent on the particular kind, or denomination, of church you attend since many individual churches seem to be able to experiment and introduce novelty, or use ancient and modern, with equal ease. This is not true of every single church, of course. Some are very steady in their commitment to a certain theology and practice of worship and stay carefully with that particular method, almost as if unaware that it represents only one element in the enormous variety present in churches today.

At a more formal institutional level, the changes that have taken place in public worship in local churches in recent decades have been accompanied by the introduction of new liturgical material by most major denominations. These new books of liturgy have reflected changing practices in the churches, but have also stimulated further variety in public worship. The manner in which such liturgical material and other new worship practices cross church boundaries is bewildering. Great creeds now jostle for space with contemporary songs, screens with surplices, prophesying with processions. In one service you might hear tongues as well as the Te Deum, icons alongside IT, and guitars with the Glorias. On the whole, all the variety and experimentation taking place in contemporary public worship must be regarded as a good thing, not least because worshippers are learning by experience to appreciate and value aspects of other Christian traditions.

The range of content in services is a response to the challenges being presented by the cultural context in which we live. Our concern here, however, is not so much with the variety and inventiveness of the public worship of the contemporary church as with the theological motivations and structure that underlie it all. Our subject is one particular dimension that seems so often to be missing: the worship of God as creator and the appreciation of his wonderful creation.

Setting the scene

Let me begin by sketching three scenes in which you may find yourself as a member of a Sunday congregation.

> In the first scene I arrive at church on a Sunday morning and sit down. The leader, after a friendly welcome, invites us with a brief introductory prayer to enter a time of worship 'because Jesus is alive' and he is to be the centre of our thoughts and adoration. She then leads into a song, which we sing enthusiastically. This gives me the words, 'I love you, Lord Jesus, you are everything to me, my heart is glad because you died for me.' The service proceeds with a similar emphasis on the gospel themes of the person of Christ, his work on the cross, his resurrection and the power of God by the Spirit to descend and to work in and upon the gathered worshippers.

Now no objection can be made to such a Christ-oriented way of entering into corporate worship. Worship should indeed be centred on Christ and should rehearse the great themes of the gospel. The people should be able to realise his risen presence, and in some way express love for Christ and commitment to him in the light of his cross and saving grace. So what is wrong with that? Its weakness is the lack of any considered concept of God as the one who creates all things and stands in sovereign relation to them. This is the significant omission of such 'evangel-centred' public worship.

> In the second scene the pastor opens the service with a statement about what is going on in the life of the church at present. He recalls the church vision and the steps that are being taken to create new structures of leadership and to engage in mission. In the opening prayer I am helped to praise God for the church and its life and for the privilege of being part of this congregation. The prayer continues by recalling some of the great times there have been recently in worship and seeking God in prayer, and inviting the Spirit to do new things among us today. The service sustains this theme of the activity of God in the church and the sermon concludes with an appeal to get more involved, to be a praying people, and to engage in the witness activities of the church.

Again you may ask what is wrong with this approach to a Sunday service. The life of the church is important and the activities of prayer and witness energise us all and give spiritual meaning to our Christian community. We are all happier, stronger and more effective when we are committed to one another and united in the corporate vision of our own church. But the weakness of such public worship is the lack of any deliberate connection to the daily lives and work of the vast majority of the congregation. It does not touch the realities and burdens of daily life. The God we worship on Sunday is not only the Lord of our church. He is not only at work in our corporate activity. He is also the creator God who is interested and active in the matters of every day. He is present in the daily lives of the people, and these things need to be represented in our corporate worship. This is the significant omission of such 'church-orientated' public worship.

> In the third scene I go to church week after week to services where the set liturgy is well prepared, has a balance of doctrine and variety of content. The services are thoughtfully led and they help me to worship and pray and seek the strength I need. There is helpful teaching and a regular beneficial offering of the Sacrament of Communion. Intercessions are always included and they cover mission and the needs of the country in its political and social dimensions. There is also prayer about world poverty and for issues of justice. The sermons share this breadth of vision of the work of God in the church and the world and the responsibility we have of living out the gospel in our lives.

There is much of value in this well-tried and much appreciated approach to public worship with its ordered and secure foundation in the liturgical tradition of the church. On a deeper consideration of this church and its pattern of services, however, there appears one very significant omission. There is never mention of what is arguably the main problem that faces the human race at present, the ecological crisis. The comparatively recent arrival of the ecological issue on the agenda of the whole world has to a large extent bypassed the church, certainly in its public worship. The set liturgies, even those framed within recent years, have hardly had time to include such matters in their texts. It takes a creative and energetic leader to find or to construct suitable material for inclusion, although it does exist, and thus its absence is perpetuated. This is the significant omission of liturgy-framed public worship.

The evidence

These three scenes are imaginative reconstructions, but they are each an accurate cameo of what actually takes place in some church services and are common in many. How can we know this? The great difficulty in making any kind of judgement about the content of worship services in churches is that you can only personally be present in one service at a time, which is hardly ground for a general view. You can study the set liturgies of the different denominations, but the question then is, to what extent are they followed, and what parts of them are being used on any given Sunday? The only sure way to study the content of worship is to look at everything that actually happens and all that is said in a service. You need to collect services and analyse them in detail.

The reconstructions above are based on an analysis of the content of over 140 weekly church services.[2] This research material consists of three groups of sources: transcripts of 91 recordings of services from a number of denominations, including different styles of worship; 28 detailed orders of service from one Anglican parish church; and a further 21 liturgies from a Roman Catholic church. These latter services of the weekly Mass were analysed from dated 'missalettes', an unofficial publication based on the Roman Missal,[3] which are used by many Catholic priests to provide a printed service for the congregation to follow, and which therefore give an accurate indication of the actual verbal content of any particular service, including the hymns and Scripture readings.

To complete the picture, the standard written liturgies of the various denominations were also examined, including the Eastern Orthodox Divine Liturgy. The latter invariably follows the set words and includes little or no informal material, so study of the printed Orthodox Divine Liturgy yields the information needed.[4]

Looking again at these three imagined examples, in what I have called 'evangel-centred' public worship there is a strong emphasis on the saving actions of God and the Christological dimensions of worship, emphasising the work of Christ on the cross, his resurrection, his lordship and reign and the gift and activity of the Holy Spirit. The doctrine of creation, however, and a vision of the humanity of Christ, are generally neglected in such services.

In other churches, and in many individual services, there is a tendency to an inward-looking focus on the local church, its vision, leaders and activities. In this 'church-orientated' worship the level of commitment to Christ is measured by attendance and involvement and the ways that members of the congregation relate to the church and its programme. This is then reflected in the verbal content of the services and results in a lack of connection between the daily lives and work of ordinary people and the content of the service. The declaration that God is creator of all things and sovereign over all life, present and at work in daily life, needs to be recovered, or strengthened, in public worship in many such churches.

In 'liturgy-framed' worship, and in fact in most services of any style, the major contemporary issue facing the planet and its occupants, ecology and the environment, is almost entirely neglected. To take only one example, in the 91 transcripts analysed there are possibly five lines where sins of abuse against the created world are acknowledged, but all these are about sin against the human creation – our fellow human beings – not the natural world. The inclusion of the line from a commonly used confession, 'we have marred your image in us', is the nearest any of these services comes to what might be called 'ecological confession'. This problem is also evident in the Anglican service orders. *Common Worship: Services and Prayers for the Church of England* does contain such prayers and lines, but of the 28 Anglican services examined, none has any ecological confession and only 3 include the line about the image of God quoted above. There is thus no penitence in these services for failure in environmental stewardship, or for wrong done to God's created order. Confession of this kind has not penetrated any of the churches studied. Some Christian pressure groups have liturgies that are devoted to the themes of ecology, creation and stewardship of the natural world, and we discuss these in more detail in Chapter 5, but the evidence collected from ordinary weekly Christian worship shows an almost total neglect of these issues.

A needed recovery

The basic proposal of this book is that a recovery of the theology of creation in relation to corporate worship is needed, along with a reassertion of the doctrine of creation in the verbal content of

Christian public worship. This is one way, the most effective way, to correct the weaknesses we have discerned. This recovery will be helped when ministers and leaders of worship acknowledge and use some kind of theological structure for public worship. It is clear that for many who lead services there is no such structure or, if there is, that it omits the doctrine of creation.

In the course of examining the 91 transcripts of recorded services, attention was paid to the opening minutes of each to see to what extent, if at all, there is reference to God as creator or to the world as his creation so as to provide a theological framework for other themes in the service. A survey of the first two pages of each service, approximately 100 lines of the transcripts, shows that 30 of the 91 services have no statement about God as creator. In some of them metaphors or images from creation occur and in that way provide such a creation context. But for all of these services, no clear statement is made about God as creator, either in prayer, reading, hymn or song, although such material may be present later in the service. There is significant variation in this respect from services based on a set liturgy or on a consciously prepared theological structure. Self-consciously prepared set liturgy does have a studied theological structure that invariably includes creation themes in the opening minutes of the service, but for one third of the service transcripts studied, no theology of creation or Creator was present at the beginning.

We may conclude, then, from looking at Christian worship in this particular way, that for many of those preparing these services no conscious theological structure for worship is conceived, or none that includes the doctrine of creation.

Preliminary points

Before we proceed, a number of preliminary points need to be clarified. First, our subject is Christian 'public worship' or 'common worship', sometimes called 'corporate worship': that is, the worship that takes place when Christians meet together to express praise and thanks to God and to engage in mutually edifying activity. The usual occasion for such worship is on Sundays in public services, although it can take place anywhere, at any time.

The precise context of our discussion is, therefore, regular public worship in any style or format.

A second point arises, however. In sustaining this focus on public worship, we do not thereby devalue other ways of conceiving the concept of worship, either theologically or practically. The New Testament writers see the whole life of the Christian believer as worship.[5] We are each to present our body, and with it our whole life, as 'a living sacrifice' to God.[6] Christians are a holy priesthood who 'offer spiritual sacrifices', and this worship is as much about honourable conduct in society as about declaring the praises of God.[7] Such a way of viewing worship is not excluded by our discussion. The result of deeper public worship should be more devoted offering of the whole of life. Consideration of the corporate dimension of Christian worship and how this may need to develop in relation to a vision of the Creator and his creation extends outwards so that the whole life of the believer is more fully an act of worship to the creator God and is lived in deeper understanding of his creation. The precise intention of this book, however, is to develop our understanding of what is happening in church, and to consider how such public worship may need to change.

Third, the discussion is about the verbal content of services rather than ritual actions or other kinds of movement, such as drama or dance. To put it another way, our discussion is first about the words that are spoken in services and then consequently about actions that are performed. Words and actions often go together, of course, so there is an inevitable link between acts and words, which needs to be recognised. More important, words usually accompany the actions and give meaning to the actions. So, for example, in the Communion service, the bread is not just set on the table, it is prayed over. It is not just broken in silence and distributed, the words of Jesus at the Last Supper are repeated and in this act an offer of grace is made. An interpretation of the act, a theology of this bread, is created by the words spoken. This is true of almost every aspect and action of public worship (although there is powerful value in silent action too). The words of the service, in readings, songs, prayers and verbal links, frame the whole in a theology and give a particular meaning to the worship event in its totality and to every part of it. So the words are important, as well as the actions, and are the first focus of our discussion.

Fourth, coming as I do from an evangelical and nonconformist tradition, I have this world of churches and their worship primarily in view. It may be the case that this particular stream of church life is more subject to the weaknesses that we have already identified – worshipping without conscious theological structure and omitting the doctrine of creation from their more informal 'liturgies'. As we have already noted, churches that do not use a set written liturgy are more prone to these problems. However, it is all too possible, even for church traditions that use set liturgy in public worship, to abandon it and to do so in a way that produces the very weaknesses of content that we are discussing. This problem is in evidence in the Anglican service transcripts examined, in which the set liturgy was used only in a very limited way. Even, however, with a set liturgy, a process of selection occurs in which certain prayers, hymns and other material are chosen and not others, which leaves the worship open to all the weaknesses we are considering. So in a contemporary Christian world where flexibility is encouraged and multiple choices are now given for services, even in denominations that have a written liturgy, there is an urgent need to become more aware of the importance of theological structure in public worship and specifically to place the worship of the saving God in proper relationship to his work as creator.

But first we need to take a deeper look at why it might be important to consider the subject of creation in public worship.

2

Knowing, Believing and Ecology

People go to church from somewhere. They go to public worship from a particular context. The context that Christians inhabit influences the way they interpret and understand what happens in church. It is important for us to examine what is happening in services of worship and our purpose is to do so with particular reference to the worship of God as creator. But we cannot discuss issues about corporate worship without examining the context in which we stand.

In this chapter we explore three aspects of the general context in which the worship of the Christian church is taking place. In the following chapter we look at two further matters that are of special relevance to the contemporary church. These may be summarised as follows.

In the general context:

- worship as a way of knowing;
- the impact of public worship on belief;
- the ecological crisis.

In the church context:

- the pastoral connection – changing a Christian's behaviour;
- the mission opportunity – connecting to unbelievers.

Worship as a way of knowing

Knowing about great bike riders and knowing how to ride a bike seem at first to be two different kinds of knowing. You might think of the first as mental knowledge and the second as experiential knowledge. But how do I come to know something? This is a question that has intrigued thinkers since the times of the earliest philosophers. Do I come to know something new because I am told it, or because I read about it in a reliable book? Or is it because I am convinced by some internal thought process that the proposition is true and believable? Or is it more complicated than that? Philosophers have now begun to say that knowing something is as much to do with me as with the new thing I have come to know. They argue that in order to know about a bike rider you need the same kind of commitment and conviction that you would need for learning to ride his bike. The same process you go through to learn to ride a bike is also taking place as you come to know about a famous bike rider.

Worship as a place of knowing

Christians have always seen this in relation to religious truth. We have spoken, for example, of knowing God personally rather than just knowing about him, of the head–heart gap, of what you know in your head needing to descend to your heart, and so on. But today even so called 'empirical science' is challenged by this new understanding since there always has to be an observer, and the observer is never just an impersonal and objective bystander, a merely rational being. The observer always interprets what they see; they are always personally involved.

Stated in more technical language, in the twentieth century there was a movement of thought over epistemology (how we come to know things). Renewed interest in the study of public worship, liturgy and ritual arises partly because of this movement of thought. If new knowledge is as much to do with my personal, committed response to what is presented as with that which is presented, then a religious or worshipful response to God must be a way to the knowledge of God. Significant ideas in this respect were explored by the Christian philosopher Paul Ricoeur (1913–2005). He approached both philosophy and the

Bible by seeing their study as primarily a task of interpreting the words of texts. But he also argued that to do so the reader needs to enter the whole narrative world of that text. He therefore stressed the inevitability of the personal commitment of the interpreter and argued that this confessional, faith perspective is basic to knowing anything.

In an essay Ricoeur describes five fundamental kinds of discourse found in the Christian Scriptures (prophetic, narrative, prescriptive, wisdom and hymnic).[1] In the hymnic discourse all the experiences of life are transformed into a second person address to God, so that God is now recognised as 'you'. The worshippers find something new happening within them as all life is expressed in words of praise, supplication and thanksgiving. In fact, a revelation occurs. Ricoeur concludes: 'The word forms our feelings in the process of expressing it. And revelation is this very formulation of our feelings that transcends their everyday ordinary modalities.'[2] He is not arguing that this is the sum total of revelation, since we have the acts of God in history and the incarnation and earthly life of Jesus as the fundamental revelation of God. But revelation by God in history needs to connect in revelation by the Spirit to the believer in the present.

Ricoeur's insight about hymnic revelation as the 'formulation of our feelings' explains in part why worship services often have such a deep effect on people. If you lead from the front and look out on a congregation, you see people in various emotional states, sometimes sitting crying, or looking up smiling, or standing with rapt attention, focused on something unseen, or at other times just seeming to be deeply at peace in the unseen presence of God. As the words are spoken out, the creed is read together, or a song expresses love for God communally, something changes. In that moment, as worshippers commit themselves in spoken words, or respond in singing, a new revelation occurs, or new knowledge is discovered. The new knowledge comes, not just earlier in the service so that after that a response can be made, thus separating the new knowledge from the response, nor later in some other part of the service, such as the sermon, when the new knowledge is seen in merely rational, intellectual terms, but as a unified experience, right then and there as the very words of worship are being spoken or sung.

All this is simply to show that acts of public worship feature today as part of a general scheme of thinking that explores how we come to know things, to know God in particular. In public worship there is a way of knowing, a way of entering a new divine world through movements of the heart, that is expressed in the public adoration of God. All public worship must be seen as deeply significant in the whole process of coming to know God and of growing in the knowledge of God. To know him, you have to get on the bike and ride right in.

Worship and imagination

We can also look at this question about the way we come to know things by starting with the subject of human imagination. If you plan a dinner date, or begin a decorating job, or just decide to take a walk round the block, you have to use your imagination. You have to picture what it will be like in order to set yourself going. Trevor Hart comments, 'It is virtually impossible to identify any human activity or capacity from which imagination is entirely absent, or in which it does not play some basic role.'[3] The problem is that a separation has existed, particularly in western Reformed theology, between reason and imagination on the basis that human imagination will lead us astray and that what is needed is the reasoned interpretation of the revelation of God, especially the written word. But in the contemporary church the place of imagination is being newly respected and is regarded as central to discovering religious truth.

Hart's specific purpose in affirming the place of imagination is to stress its importance in living in the experience of the Christian hope.[4] His words apply equally, however, to the whole process of corporate worship. God is able to seize our imagination, not just our mind and will. When we hear God's promise, we have to use our imagination to begin to see his offered future. We then come to believe that such a future is possible and, as we do so, he draws us forward into new experience of his presence and action. Such a process is what is taking place in public worship. Take, for example, a led prayer of penitence. The person leading expresses contrition for sins in a general way and then says in the prayer, 'So, holy Father, we come to you as the leper, kneeling before you and saying, "If you will, you can make me clean." We hear your words of healing, "I will. Be clean." And we feel the touch of your hand. Remove from our lives all that is not holy and pure. Thank you, Lord Jesus. Amen.'

In this simple way, and in many similar moments in public worship, the glorious world of God and his gospel is set out. The prayers, songs and actions display this eternal world and, as it is grasped by the imagination of the worshippers, become the means by which they 're-imagine' their present lives as well as their eternal future. The person who is not yet a believer may find that such imagining in worship is the beginning of faith.

The contemporary Christian, who lives in an alien society, finds through regular attendance at public worship that their life is continually reordered and moulded by the world of God, which is imagined in that worship. The recovery of imagination as a central aspect of what is happening in public worship is a key to understanding its importance. Worship is important not only for the development of the individual Christian believer, which tends to be stressed, but also for the health of the community around the church and for society at large.

This idea that public worship is the place where God is known is nothing new to the church. This theology appears in some form in all the main traditions. It is there in Psalm 73, where the troubled man complains of the injustice and bitterness of life, and the mood of the psalm changes as he says, 'until I went into the sanctuary of God'. In communal worship he is held in new security, finds new strength, and is 'near God'.[5] This theology is there in the Reformed tradition, which sees in the power of the word preached publicly 'the clear manifestation of the mystery of Christ'.[6] It is there also in the sacramental traditions, which stress the real presence of Christ in the Eucharist so that you come to know Christ more deeply by participation in the acts of worship. In the Eastern Orthodox churches in particular you know the mystery of God through worship more than through reason. The great theologians of the East are monks and saints rather than academics because philosophy begins from faith[7] and personal and rational knowledge are not distinguished.[8]

So if the idea that knowing God through acts of public worship is not new, why is it now important? It is because, as we have shown, the wider secular context has begun to reconsider such personal engagement as a significant way of knowing. The Christian understanding about knowing God in worship has therefore begun to resonate in new ways with the same thinking in society. There is a new mood in which public worship is regarded positively as a primary means for the knowledge of God for the whole world. There is therefore great value in Christians considering this theme again, and casting a critical eye over what takes place in public worship. In particular, in the light of our concerns about the doctrine of creation, we can look at how far the knowledge of God as creator is discovered in worship and how the worshipper is helped to engage with such a God and with his marvellous creation.

The impact of public worship on belief

A second aspect of the general context in which Christians are going to church is a renewed interest in the relationship between public worship and doctrine. Under this heading we are thinking not so much about the general idea of knowing God through ways other than intellectual engagement as about the shaping of people's specific beliefs through their attendance at public worship. This relationship is often expressed in the Latin tag *lex orandi, lex credenda* (the law of praying is the law of believing). In other words, what you believe and what you pray are intimately connected – the one influences the other.

As already noted, integrating thinking or writing about doctrine with worship, both public and private, is the fundamental understanding of how theology works in the Eastern tradition. The concept was summarised by Evagrios, a fourth-century monk who lived many years in the Egyptian desert: 'If you are a theologian you will truly pray, if you truly pray you will be a theologian.'[9] This deep relationship between worship and doctrine is expressed repeatedly in recent theological writing, which recognises that 'worship is embodied theology'.[10] The mutual influence of corporate worship and Christian doctrine is a developing discussion in the contemporary church and is 'likely to be a subject of lively debate for some time to come'.[11]

The influence of public worship

The study and analysis of corporate worship is therefore important because its influence on the beliefs of the worshippers through the liturgical orders and texts may be more powerful than official statements of belief. With the exception of the classical creeds, which are said regularly in some traditions, statements of faith tend to be kept for reference and theological discussion rather than being repeated in public services. You might say, 'Well, we have the sermon, which is also part of the worship.' This is true, and doctrinal teaching from the Bible has a central place in most Christian worship. However, we more easily remember and absorb what we repeat often. Public teaching is usually not repetitious and is thus less memorable. I suspect that you can remember many, many prayers and hymns, but very few sermons. Liturgies, in contrast to sermons, are more widely disseminated and used, and become the common language of faith for Christian communities. Luther's liturgical writing became a vehicle for his reforming doctrine.

> Few of his writings became as influential and were reported as often as the liturgical orders published under his name. They passed into the church orders of the Reformation and became normative for Lutheran worship.
>
> (*Ulrich Leupold*, Luther's Works)[12]

This influence is equally true of 'non-liturgical' church orders. In the Pentecostal churches, for example, there is an 'oral liturgy' of hymns, songs, prayers and other material constantly in use.[13] Such liturgy has as much influence as written liturgy or written doctrine. So Hollenweger remarks that 'hymns are more decisive in their influence on the religious beliefs and practices of Pentecostals than is the literature of the Pentecostal movement'.[14] The theological vision by which most believers live is therefore deeply influenced by the words that are said or sung in worship in both written and informal liturgy. Things that are habitually and repeatedly said are especially influential on belief, whether or not the vision of God created by these words is the same as that of official creeds, or classical texts.[15]

Worship and emotion

A further factor strengthens this point. Changes in Christian thinking brought about by corporate worship have deep impact because of the inherent emotional nature of worship, and these changes are continually sustained and strengthened by habitual and repeated practice. In the case of hymns and songs, a musician and hymn writer of a former age wrote,

> A congregation's disposition towards right belief or away from it is subtly influenced by the habitual use of hymns. No single influence in public worship can so surely condition a congregation to self-deception, to fugitive follies, to religious perversities, as thoughtlessly chosen hymns. The singing congregation is uncritical; but it matters very much what it sings, for it comes to believe its hymns. Wrong doctrine in preaching would be noticed; in hymns it may come to be believed.
>
> (*Eric Routley*, Hymns Today and Tomorrow)[16]

Here Routley points out that the influence of hymn singing in public worship may be for good doctrine, or for bad. The same point may be made of present worship, sung or spoken. The emotional and uncritical nature of the worship experience means that doctrinal imbalance or error is difficult to perceive and difficult to correct. The worship service in its totality influences the beliefs of the ordinary Christian unawares. In educational terms this is called the 'hidden curriculum' and it is more influential on behaviour than the 'manifest curriculum'.[17] One noted educationist says,

> We learn all the time. My conviction is that this hidden curriculum, this subconscious learning, is so important we cannot afford to let it remain unconscious. We need to look at the total learning experience of people and bring as many aspects as possible into conscious, deliberate, systematic, and sustained efforts.
>
> (*John H. Westerhoff*, A Colloquy on Christian Education)[18]

We have to conclude that for the ordinary believer contemporary theology is being formed by public worship, for good or ill. Part of the problem is that in many services imbalance or neglect exists in worship with regard to the doctrine of creation, to say nothing of other aspects of Christian doctrine. To write or to preach about it is no doubt useful, but the doctrine of creation may more effectively be recovered for the ordinary believer through paying attention to its place in public worship. This is basically the argument of this book.

Which comes first?

But do Christian worship services not reflect doctrine rather than form it? If you are preparing and leading a service, you do it on the basis of previously held doctrinal convictions. You believe in the deity of Christ, the presence of the Spirit, the priority of Christian love and the effectiveness of the grace of God and so on, and you prepare your songs and prayers and sermon with these doctrines in mind. Even without conscious reference to your beliefs, they influence what you prepare. This is certainly the case. But any minister or leader has already been deeply instructed by the 'hidden curriculum' of their own church and the habits of speech and action in the services. You do not come to settled convictions about doctrine without the context of the corporate worship that you have experienced, perhaps from your very earliest days. Karl Barth, in a rare written recollection of his childhood, shows the influence of worship on doctrinal belief. Writing about a collection of children's songs that he sang as a child, he says,

> This was the text-book in which . . . I received my first theological instruction in a form appropriate to my then immaturity. And what made an indelible impression on me was the homely naturalness with which these very modest compositions spoke about the events of Christmas, Palm Sunday, Good Friday, Easter, the Ascension and Pentecost.
>
> (*Karl Barth*, Church Dogmatics)[19]

This all illustrates the complex question of the relative priority of worship and doctrine in the theological task. Which comes first, theology or worship? Different solutions to this problem have been found in the history of the church. The first possible solution is to say that the expression in corporate gatherings of adoration, praise and thanksgiving to God in response to his activity in the world precedes doctrinal formulation. In this case worship is primary and theology secondary.[20] Augustine uses the practice of infant baptism to offer grounds for his concept of original sin, prioritising liturgical practice over theology.[21] Some speak of worship as the primary source and stimulus of Christian theology, and so they call worship 'primary theology' and theological reflection 'secondary theology'.[22]

If, however, we move from worship practice to doctrinal conviction, we may be in danger of creating a mystical or incoherent set of doctrines based thoughtlessly on the accumulated habits of a given church. One example of the weakness of this approach might be the repeated invitations in some church traditions to 'claim your healing from God tonight'. This statement, and others like it, regularly included in services, create the belief that anyone, at any time of life, or in any situation, has a right to expect to be healed of any illness. This is manifestly untrue, both in terms of Jesus' ministry and in terms of our understanding of God's general ways of working. There are better and more pastorally helpful ways of saying what needs to be said in respect of God's healing power.

Or take the practice of regularly praying for those who have died, in the sense that they can be aided by our prayers to progress into heaven. Such a practice encourages belief that there is an opportunity beyond death for progress to full eternal life, or to correct inadequate faith in this life. But the teaching of Jesus seems to promise full salvation and God's presence after death for those who believe, and the New Testament writers are clear that through Christ there is eternal life like his and with him. The habits of a church at worship create a theology that may not be easy to criticise or to change, simply because they are ingrained habits.

In the second possible solution, previously constructed theological beliefs have been widely used to critique practices in worship and liturgical habits. For the professional theologian or church leader, as opposed to the ordinary believer, giving theology priority over worship in the theological method is almost inevitable. One of the two primary motivations for the sixteenth-century Reformation, according to Calvin, was the recovery of

pure public worship of God as judged by a biblical theology[23]
More cautiously, Carson indicates that we must judge corporate
worship not by biblical theology, seen as various theological
insights from different parts of the Bible, but by systematic theology informed by Scripture.[24] We can then take a broad view of
what the Bible as a whole says about worship and also learn from
the way that it has been understood by the church down the centuries. The danger of using previously constructed theological
schemes to critique public worship is that we merely develop a
habit of careful definition rather than spiritual worship and such
schemes have often led to arid doctrinal controversy.[25]

The relative place of doctrine and worship in the theological
method is thus a difficult question to resolve. A way through,
however, may be found in a 'doxological method', that is, in seeing that Christian worship is inextricably linked to doctrine and
that the place of communal adoration in the presence of God is
where theological reflection best takes place.[26] We have noted that
the Eastern Orthodox Churches have always stressed this
approach. The weekly Sunday liturgy is the centre of life for
Orthodox believers.

The literal meaning of 'Orthodox' is simply 'right glorifying'.
The title reflects the belief that theology, or right believing, cannot be separated from communal worship, or right glorifying, of
God. This is because God is known to us, not primarily in a
rational relationship since in his eternal being he is ultimate mystery beyond the grasp of human minds, but is available to the
human senses.[27] The first and greatest way that this knowledge of
God is made possible is through the historic coming of Christ the
Word in his incarnation, and then, in the present, by believers'
contemplation of him, and refreshed union with him through the
Holy Spirit in the weekly celebration of the Eucharist. On the
basis of such continual contemplation of Christ Orthodox theology is done. This is the doxological method.

Scripture and doctrine

A further aspect of this deep relationship between doctrine and
worship may be seen in the idea that corporate worship is
the best place for working out the relationship of Scripture and
theology. In his Old Testament theology Walter Brueggemann

develops the concept that Israel's testimony about God, recorded in many forms in the Old Testament, is fundamental to her special place in the world.[28] He links this 'testimony' in part to corporate thanksgiving, and therefore to Israel's practice of worship. So the psalms, and other portions of Scripture that are clearly set within, or are used in, the liturgy of the nation's worship become a starting point for expressing their theology.[29] Brueggemann then applies this same principle to the way the church might engage in her theological thinking. He calls for a tension to be maintained between biblical study and theology and comments, 'In practice it is the liturgy that is to enact the settled coherence of the church's faith, and the sermon that provides the "alien" witness of the text, which rubs against the liturgic coherence.'[30]

Brueggemann is pointing out that the prayers, readings and songs of public worship are the way the church expresses in regular practice the longer held and more generally accepted doctrines. The sermon, or the teaching element of the worship, is then an opportunity to challenge those beliefs, or to bring new insight and application from Scripture. This is a very helpful way in which we might think about the relationship of the 'praying' and the 'teaching' aspects of public worship. Both are needed and they help us to hold firm to the doctrines that are dear to us while at the same time giving room for challenge and new applications. Here is the Christian community at work, in the context of worship, framing and sustaining its doctrine. It is in this way that worship and doctrine are truly related.

We may conclude that corporate worship, as it sums up and expresses the settled theology of the church, must be seen as profoundly influencing the continuing doctrinal understanding of believers. It therefore also has a strong effect on the way that worshipping believers live out their Christian faith. But public worship must also be consistently criticised and reshaped on the basis of theological discussion and thinking. It is our purpose to attempt something of this work. We are asking if the church at worship needs more clearly to express her faith in God the Father as creator of heaven and earth, in his Son as the one in whom all things hold together and towards whom all things are moving, and in the Spirit who indwells the creation and is perfecting it. These matters have a new urgency in the light of the issue to be discussed next: the ecological crisis that the world now faces.

The ecological crisis

The present environmental crisis was perceived by some long before the twentieth century.[31] The nineteenth-century art critic and romantic John Ruskin, for example, noted the effect of industrial pollution on his much-loved mosses in his Lake District garden on the edge of Coniston Water. He was one of the first to suggest that air pollution would cause a rise in the temperature of the atmosphere. A far-sighted prediction, as it has turned out. Environmental issues present the contemporary church with an increasing challenge and they have direct relevance to the doctrine of creation and to the questions about public worship under our investigation.

The historical roots

Lynn White, in a controversial article, proposed that the Christian doctrine of human dominion over creation drawn from Genesis 1 is the underlying cause of the ecological problems of the western world. He calls for a rejection of 'the Christian axiom that nature has no reason for existence but to serve man'.[32] This criticism is to some extent a misunderstanding of Christian teaching and also ignores the universal factors of arrogant human behaviour that have created the crisis.[33] But though White's idea has to a large extent been answered by careful Christian responses,[34] we need to acknowledge that since the sixteenth-century Reformation there has in fact been an emphasis in the 'Christian' industrialised west on the dominion of humankind over creation. It may have been misguided, driven more by secular motives and commercial greed than by theological conviction, but it was present none the less. Such a view arises easily where human beings and God are defined primarily by their relationship to each other and not by their relationship to 'nature' or the created world. Individual faith, personal moral progress and a way into eternal life was the great programme of the reformers. Such a theological scheme, the purpose of which is to enable the secure relationship of a human being to God and the progress of that relationship, 'not only frees both of them for history, it also makes nature itself available for man's use'.[35] A conviction about the God-given right of humanity to use the earth's resources is a recognised factor in the commercial development of the western world, but it has profound environmental consequences and continues to influence the present attitudes and ecological behaviour of Christians.[36]

A theological answer

We need to accept, as Lynn White and others have argued, that aspects of religious belief in recent centuries, or their practical outcomes built on faulty theology, have contributed to our ecological problems.[37] If this is so, then it encourages us to begin by looking for a religious and therefore a theological answer to the environmental questions facing the world. As White says, 'Since the roots of our trouble are so largely religious, the remedy must be essentially religious, whether we call it that or not.'[38]

The 'ecological doctrine of creation'

One theological response to this challenge is the 'ecological doctrine of creation', a serious attempt by the German theologian Jürgen Moltmann to correct the criticised dominion theology. He recognises the 'apocalyptic' crisis that faces humanity and acknowledges that this situation demands that Christians make new theological responses. His particular contribution is to argue for a strengthened understanding of the presence of God by the Spirit in his creation where 'the centre is the recognition of the presence of God *in* the world and the presence of the world *in* God'.[39] Moltmann stresses the intimate relationship of the Creator to his created world and the responsibility of humanity for that world in which God is present by his Spirit.

We have already emphasised the profound relationship of theology and worship. If it is indeed the case that public worship functions to form and change people's beliefs, as well as to express them, then a response to the new context of ecological concern must be not just creative theological writing, but liturgical change. The church cannot ignore its wider context and still be faithful to God's call. The cultural context (in this case the environmental challenges we face) has raised questions about Christian theology and thus questions about the shape and content of our public worship. The Christian church cannot stand aloof.

Our story in ritual

Two writers on Christian worship have explored this matter. Geoffrey Wainwright draws on insights from anthropology to suggest that a significant role be given to ritual activity in maintaining order within a social universe. In this understanding ritual activity puts each generation in touch with 'an archetypal story' that accounts for the present order of the society and of the world in general. So in many societies the ritual rehearsal of the original creative event plays a significant part in the continuance of that society's well-being.[40] He argues that because of the environmental crisis we face, the church needs to respond in new ways – it needs to be 'reinvented'.[41]

From his Methodist sacramental convictions, Wainwright then looks for a renewed approach to ritual activity through baptism and the Eucharist.[42] Implicit in these Christian sacramental actions are the story of creation, the value and sacredness of created things and the blessing of their gift. The actions performed with the elements of water and bread and wine could, he says, be signs of a new approach to creation. But explanations about the created things being used (in this case, bread and water) do not follow in the liturgy. Nor are the implications for a doctrine of creation made clear in the words that accompany the actions, or surround them in the rest of the service. This is of course right, since in the services of baptism and Eucharist the focus is not primarily on creation but on the saving power of God in Christ. In these actions God works to bring about new creation, to save by atoning blood and to sustain with 'the bread of life'. The great story of creation, as seen in the Creator's providence for, presence in and consummation of, the material world he has created, while implicit and perhaps briefly stated in the Eucharist, needs to be expressed in a broader way than the sacramental actions envisaged by Wainwright. The story of God, set out in the service as a whole, and his creating and sustaining of the natural world presented more deliberately in liturgy, is a needed Christian response to the ecological crisis.

Our worship reflecting culture

The second theological response with implications for public worship comes from John Witvliet. He discusses the question of how the cultural context impacts Christian worship.[43] This is the process of liturgical inculturation, a commonly understood process by which the worship of a church gradually reflects the cultural factors present in the society. The most obvious example is the transference of musical styles from the society to the church, justified in the famous quotation attributed to General Booth, founder of the Salvation Army: 'Why should the devil have all the best music?'

Inculturation is also the source of the commonly experienced 'worship wars' of the local church. One of Witvliet's key conclusions is that 'the relationship between liturgy and culture is theologically framed by the biblical-theological categories of creation and incarnation'.[44] He argues that the ability of a particular church to engage with its local culture is directly proportionate to the value it places on creation. Devaluing creation, or subordinating it to redemption in a theological scheme, produces scepticism about cultural engagement. Or the opposite may be the case – placing a high value on creation increases the possibility of engagement in the culture. In this case the culture is viewed by the church, at least to some extent, in a positive light and points of contact with it are seen. This positive relationship is then reflected in services by the inclusion of culturally appropriate forms and style.[45]

Witvliet's argument here is primarily about the inculturation that may take place in services by the incorporation of *style and forms* of worship appropriate to the cultural context. But the same argument may be made about *content* in services, that is, about the things that are said and sung. We are arguing that the context of environmental concern needs to be inculturated into liturgy by a more robust presence of the doctrine of creation. Witvliet's view of the relationship between liturgy and culture outlined above – that it is 'framed by the biblical-theological categories of creation and incarnation' – certainly applies to Christian public worship, so that the church adapts its forms and style, but it also applies to the doctrinal content. A reconsideration of the basic frame of creation, within which the great subject of redemption is set during Christian public worship, is an appropriate and much-needed response to the challenge of the environmental crisis.

We need to note that inculturation, in the way we have discussed it, is not just about a particular local church responding to environmental concerns in its immediate context. Ecology and the environment are now global issues, and therefore the need to extend the theological frame in which worship takes place challenges churches in all places. In some streams of church life Christian people have already begun to make a response in this way and more has been done in recent years in many churches. Liturgical practices that incorporate new dimensions of the doctrine of creation are being developed and these will be examined and discussed. The manner in which this is happening provides some of the material for our study and will be raised in Chapter 5. More important, the way that some of these new practices are justified theologically needs to be looked at carefully and understood, and that is part of the purpose of this book.

In conclusion, the general theological and social context in which Christian public worship is taking place impacts it deeply and affects what is happening in churches. For an example, we can take the apparently superficial argument over worship that is very likely to be happening in your church at this very moment: the complaint about not including enough 'good old hymns' in a service or, conversely, not enough 'exciting new songs'. This argument is often viewed as merely an argument about preferences: 'I like hymns, you like songs, let's agree to differ.' But if we think more carefully about it and listen to those who are able thoughtfully to explain their views, we find that the argument is exactly about the three things that we have been discussing in this chapter: how we come to know things, the relationship between worship and doctrine, and the impact of the wider social context on the church.

The song-singers stress that knowing God is about more than rational processes and want to include 'mood songs' in public worship that encourage the spiritual process to happen. So they are disappointed if there is no such opportunity in the service.

The hymn-singers stress that we need to worship with our minds and with some kind of doctrinal integrity, and, they say, 'The old hymns contain more truth in a single verse than all these self-centred devotional songs.' Both, in a strange contradiction, are responding to the social context in which some people are seeking deeper roots in history and in strong traditions – represented in church by older and well-tried hymns – while others want to go with the times and seek 'fresh expressions' and experiences – represented in church by songs recently written and in contemporary style. Granted that the third point here is not precisely about the specifics of environmental concerns, it nevertheless illustrates the impossibility of separating what is happening in the social context from the worship of the church. Nor, even while we hold fast to what is good, should we think of doing so.

3

Worship, Behaviour and Mission

In the last chapter we looked at three issues in the general contemporary context that are affecting the way that we think about the church as it is regularly at worship. In this chapter we consider two further issues in connection with public worship that are more obviously of close interest to Christians and always have been: the pastoral connection and the mission opportunity. The ordinary person 'in the pew' in church on Sunday might justifiably ask what the relevance is of discussion about worship, and the way that people come to know things, to the environmental crisis. What has all this to do with Christians seeking to live out their faith? How does it affect their behaviour and, in particular, how does it affect their daily response to the present environmental challenge?

The answer to these questions is, as I have already argued, that believers are influenced in specific beliefs by the impact of particular things that are said and done in weekly worship. These beliefs then mould accompanying attitudes and these are worked out in the accumulated habits of every day. This is the pastoral connection to public worship. The role of the worship of the church as a means of mission is a further dimension of the same process. Public services of worship may have as much influence on the person of little or no faith as on the one who is already a believer. But this only happens if the content of that worship is making some connection to the people as human beings in the actual world that they inhabit. This is the missional opportunity for Christian public worship.

The pastoral connection – changing a Christian's behaviour

Our discussion so far has been primarily about attitudes to God's creation and ecology and about ways that Christian public worship may need to change in the light of new thinking. The ultimate outcome we are looking for, however, is not about merely making changes to services but is about helping to change people's beliefs and behaviour and to sustain them in good habits of life. Through liturgical change there should be ethical change, an adaptation of Christian behaviour and an influence on habits with regard to ecology. This leads us to consider the pastoral challenge for the church in its public worship.

The lunatic fringe?

Let me begin by recounting a story about a woman who regularly attended our country Baptist church in Sussex. Although it was not her real name, she was happy to be known as 'Miss Woodland' because of her love for the nearby countryside. She was often seen out in the lanes and fields collecting berries and flowers for herself or to give to other people. She was a believer in Christ and became a member of our church. Some time later she wrote to resign her membership in protest that I, as the pastor, did not ever preach about animals. At the time, although I held her in great affection and she continued to offer many kindnesses to me and my family and to others, I thought she was just strange, someone on the lunatic fringe of the Christian church, who did not see the larger priorities of Christian truth.

But today, after many years, and with further reflection on this incident, I think that in fact Miss Woodland was making a very substantial point and was acting in accord with deeply held convictions. I now see that she was objecting not so much to the specific neglect of animals in sermons, but at a deeper level. The animal objection was merely a symbol of something larger that she discerned. She sensed, quite rightly as I now see it, that something very important was missing. She saw a whole Christian scheme which, in the process of stressing the saving history of the Bible and the need for redemption through Christ, led to neglect of the doctrine of creation, the world God has created, that he has given us to enjoy and care for (including the animals), and to which we are deeply related as created beings. She lived in a world like this herself, not first a world of church and of prayer meetings and self-conscious 'spiritual' activities. She wanted Sunday worship and preaching to be connected to the things that occupied her in daily life and interested her: the world of God's creation, its flora and fauna, and the enjoyment and responsible use of them. At the time no one was listening, so she resigned.

I hope I would listen more carefully today. The church in general certainly needs to do so and it is a point that is being made ever more loudly in a number of ways. One of the stated aims of R.J. Berry's 1997–8 Glasgow Gifford Lectures was 'to seek a robust basis for behaviour in a crowded and ill-treated world'.[1] The overall purpose of his lectures and subsequent book was to explore the relationship between religion and the natural world, and to make a contribution to a 'theology of nature'. However, the crowded and ill-treated world needs human beings not only to engage in theological discussion but, as Berry argues, to adopt whole new ethical patterns of behaviour. He quotes the World Conservation Strategy statement, which says,

> An ethic is important because what people do depends on what they believe. Widely shared beliefs are often more powerful than government edicts. The transition to sustainable societies will require changes in how people perceive each other, other life and the Earth; how they evaluate their needs and priorities and how they behave.
> (*World Conservation Strategy,* Caring for the Earth)[2]

The theology is vital and is one component in the process of change, but through 'the formative influence of the frequent corporate worship of God',[3] church leaders and leaders of worship may greatly assist Christian disciples to lead lives that affect both their own general behaviour and the environment that they inhabit.

Discipleship

Christian discipleship not only affects attitudes to the natural environment, of course, but is about the whole of life lived out in a variety of contexts and relationships. This is a primary consideration of this book: the connections that exist in public worship to the whole of life lived as created beings. So when we discuss the relationship between worship and attitudes to creation, we touch on a range of wider issues quite apart from any ecological responsibility that may be encouraged. Believers live all the time in the created worlds of work, leisure, family life, political and social involvement, and they have to work out their discipleship in every one of these areas. The ability of those who prepare and lead worship to relate the content of services both to life in general and to the demands of the kingdom of God and the ethics of Christ, is to a large extent dependent on a wide doctrinal view that includes a robust doctrine of creation. Such worship needs to include the perspective that Miss Woodland yearned for in coming to church week by week and found absent. Her objection still needs to be heard.

Worship and life

It is commonly observed that in the developed world the connection between church worship and the daily life of Christian believers has been poor. We shall look in a moment at some ways in which this weakness is being rectified. One clergyman, comparing the experience of a visit to Kenya with his own observation of church worship in the UK, writes,

> Within my experience of the work of my local parish church, there is an air of illusion in our work within the world. Going to church does not feel that God and the world are meeting in an immediate relationship. I still experience the world being left at the door even though we do speak out and take a prophetic stance in our context.
>
> (*K. Trivasse*, 'My pinching shoes')[4]

In a Baptist context, in the last century Ernest Payne regarded the weakening of convictions about public worship and the loss of good habits in the liturgy of the church in the early twentieth century as the primary reason why churches in the western world had made 'so slight an impact on individuals and communities'.[5] In a more recent study, Robin Gill argues that for Christian discipleship there is a direct correlation between attendance at regular weekly worship and the individual believer taking on some distinctive features of ethical behaviour.[6]

In a significant survey exploring the reasons why people have stopped attending church in the UK in recent years, Richter and Francis present figures on 'church leavers' and their responses to the worship of the church. The largest figures in this category come under the statement, 'The church failed to connect with the rest of my life', which was agreed by 62 per cent of people under 20, and 40 per cent of those over 20 who had left church.[7] These figures show quite convincingly that people who come to public worship have an expectation that the worship will connect widely with their lives. A high proportion of the individuals surveyed clearly did not find that this wider purpose of the church at worship was being fulfilled, so they stopped coming. It seems that in recent decades there has been a marked disconnection between worship and the daily lives of the worshippers, which pastors and leaders of worship still need to note and act upon. Richter and Francis conclude that 'one of the key responses churches could make to the cultural changes we have explored is to increase the diversity of their programmes, especially their diet of worship'.[8]

Richter and Francis also recommend that recurring patterns in worship should 'include attitudes of reverence for and enjoyment of the life of this planet'.[9] The disconnecting of public worship from the daily world that the worshippers inhabit is not a new problem. It hides an underlying theological conflict that has occupied Christian communities and great thinkers of the past, and continues today. One might summarise this conflict as the difference between seeing Christ's call (or 'vocation') to be a disciple as a call to withdrawal from the world, or as a call to fresh engagement with the world. Some monastic communities, for example, stress the need for withdrawal into a life of prayer, while others stress a life of service to the community. Martin Luther strongly challenged the idea that the Christian call separates the believer from the world of work and normal society. He insisted that God calls Christians to live in the ordinary world with a sense of his presence under, or within, the normal duties and events of life. He taught that God sustains the natural world he has created and protects it from forces that would oppose it.

Christians are therefore just as obedient to the fullness of Christ's call as they carry out their daily work, order their family life and serve in social roles, as they are when engaged in the more obviously religious observances of prayer and worship. This, he said, is the way we serve God – by serving our neighbour. Luther was firmly on the side of those who see the relationship of worship and work as fundamental to the Christian vocation.[10]

John Calvin worked from a similar understanding of the continuing presence and creative work of the Holy Spirit in the whole of life. As the inner life of the whole creation, the Spirit gives life to, and sustains, all God's creatures so the believer's daily vocation may also be viewed as 'in the Spirit'.[11] Some influential recent thinkers have sought to recover this concept. We have already noted the ideas of Jürgen Moltmann in his 'ecological theology' in which he sees the presence of the Spirit as the answer to the diminishing sense of the sacred in the created world.[12] He argues elsewhere that Christians need to understand more deeply that the Holy Spirit, who creates and energises all things, is at work in all the activities of life, way beyond the programmes of the churches. The Spirit shows himself in human love of life, his energies are the very energies of natural life and he is the one who makes all life holy 'with the Creator's passion for the life of what he has created'.[13]

If this is the way we see the work of the Spirit, then it is bound to affect the way Christians live out daily life at work and in the community. A former colleague of mine was often quoted as saying to his students: 'So does what happens at 11 o'clock on a Sunday morning make any difference to what happens at 11 o'clock on a Monday morning?'[14] In other words, are worship and work integrated? Pastors and leaders of worship are failing miserably if the answer to that question is, 'No, worship makes no difference.' Public worship ceases to have meaning if it makes no impact on daily life.

Worship and work

As a result of challenges such as these there has been a flurry of activity on the practical outcomes of public worship on daily work. Practical responses to this critique of worship are represented in the United States, for example, by the work of Robert

Banks and David Rowe. Banks emphasises the relationship between God's work and ours to enable the believer to live out the Christian life in the workplace and to deepen the connections between work and faith.[15] Rowe stresses the sacredness of work in God's plan for creation and, for the disciples who seeks to live in the kingdom of God, the need to unite worship and work.[16] In the UK recent thinking about the connection between worship and work is being done by Mark Greene.[17] The London Institute of Contemporary Christianity has developed a whole scheme to challenge the disjunction of worship and work. Through lectures and the publication of its journal *Workwise*, the Institute seeks 'to resource people for fruitful work, ministry, witness and social transformation in their workplaces'.[18]

So what has all this to do with the content of public worship? It is the question asked by my colleague, mentioned above: 'What has 11 o'clock on a Sunday morning to do with 11 o'clock on Monday morning?' It is about the effect that Sunday services have on the daily discipleship of the Christian. It is about the integrating of creation and redemption in both worship and discipleship. And in this respect, two important lessons can be learned.

Minds and actions

First, because minds may need to be changed, there may need to be theological adjustment to the content of public worship. Edmund Larive is right when he suggests that there are 'deep theological reasons why work remains a stepchild, in the church' and adds that the missing ingredient in the present Christian understanding of work is the doctrine of creation.[19] It is important to include in services aspects of the worship of the creator God, as well as worship of the saving God. All the thinkers we have discussed above stress that God's creating and redeeming activity cannot be separated, but need to be theologically integrated. God saves the world through Christ, but he is involved deeply with his world, as the sovereign Creator, as the Holy Spirit who gives life to all living things and who makes sacred the normal matters of every day.

Discipleship is partly about a Christian's mindset towards created things, and this includes the tasks of daily work, the joys of leisure, the responsibilities of home and family and duty towards the environment. The deliberate incorporation of aspects of the theology of creation in public worship broadens theological understanding of God's ways. It is one way of reversing the disconnection of worship and work and of enabling integrated discipleship.

Second, an ethical dimension is needed in Christian public worship. Not only minds, but behaviour needs to change. The deliberate inclusion in corporate worship of matters that affect the lifestyle, ethics and behaviour of worshippers cannot be done without making a fundamental connection with the doctrine of creation. Simple ways of doing this are regularly to include in services items about people's daily work or other duties – and not just the teachers, medical people and missionaries in the congregation, as so often happens. Leaders can encourage public prayer for daily work and the life situations of the congregation, and make time in services to include testimony about how someone's faith works out in the workplace. If such matters are included, then the church will offer one significant answer to those who say that the world is left at the door of the church, or that the Sunday service is irrelevant to their life.

Only last Sunday, as I write, the Sunday service I attended began with the leader inviting the congregation to leave outside 'all the things that have occupied us during the week and to focus on God'. This kind of remark is exactly the opposite of what the church needs in worship, and is contrary to all I have been arguing here. Quite apart from the possible pastoral insensitivity of such a statement, Christian disciples have the inestimable privilege of bringing all that they have experienced during the week to a God who loves them: their sins to be forgiven, their burdens to be eased, their decisions to be confirmed and their joys to be celebrated. The world is not to be boxed up quietly while we worship 'in the Spirit', but laid out so that we may see it rightly in the light of God and find liberation to serve him in it.

We might now ask, 'But does all this work?' We need to find out what evidence there is to show that the content of public worship actually has any effect on the behaviour and discipleship of the worshippers. Two final perspectives on this subject are worth considering.

Change through overwhelming

One of these is to think about attendance at public worship as an event that moves people in deeper ways than any other experience. This might be expected. If worship together with others is a unique means of encounter with the true and living God, which is the Christians' claim, then it may be assumed that joining in public worship changes people in some way. There are no doubt some who sit in church week by week who inwardly resist God's presence and do not wish to be changed at all. But for the majority, pastors and leaders of worship have a serious responsibility to see that what they plan and lead enables such encounter and does not inhibit it. As Christians living in a society where God's presence is not acknowledged, and his ways often opposed, we need the weekly encounter to help to sustain faith and obedience.

Corporate worship is intended to impact our lives. Paul Santmire speaks of 'the experience of communal ecstasy' that takes place in public worship, which changes attitudes so people act more responsibly towards the environment.[20] David Ford uses another term for this experience when he describes the prophet Ezekiel with his extraordinary visions as being 'overwhelmed' in his experience of God. He goes on to suggest that contemporary Christians living in a secular and sinful world are 'in the midst of multiple overwhelmings' and says that 'we need wisdom for coping with that . . . we are created to be overwhelmed – by God, by creation, by beauty, goodness, truth and love'.[21] He argues, therefore, that Christians need 'practices of excess' that will help them to be strong in the often overwhelming 'godless' experiences of daily life, and that some of these practices should be extreme. Like Ezekiel, who was prone to the extraordinary in both his visions and his prophetic actions, Christians may need to learn to practise the extraordinary in order to be impacted deeply by God so they can live in his way. Ford's example is the use of the Bible in which Christians need to be immersed in order to deeply inhabit the text. He says,

> We should not underestimate the erosion of Christian imagination and understanding that is taking place, even among faithful churchgoers, because of the flood of powerful ideas, images and stories that wash over us daily. In the face of such excesses the

least we need is a practice of excess that gives some chance of us being shaped even more comprehensively, imaginatively and intelligently by biblical ideas, images and stories.

(*David Ford*, 'Coping with being overwhelmed')[22]

This idea of public worship as influential upon imagination, in this case through excessive exposure to the Bible, is a very appropriate response to the challenge of a godless society, a world that does not believe in, or take account of, its Creator. It is in the context of public worship that such 'overwhelming' may be both expected and encouraged and the Christian vision of the Creator be most vividly connected to the world in which the disciple lives and works. Corporate worship is expected to do something to those who share in it together – to change them, to enable full and robust discipleship. To help that to happen in services is simply to be pastorally responsible.

Changing a world-view

In the second perspective on the pastoral and discipleship dimensions of this subject, we look at some evidence that addresses the question, 'Does such experience of God in corporate worship in fact affect worshippers' attitudes to the environment?' This is a difficult question to answer. One definition of what it means to be a 'green' Christian is: 'a complete attitude of mind, living more thoughtfully, living as God would have us live and not simply adopting the standards of the consumer society around us'.[23]

A mission statement from Earth Ministry in Seattle reads,

> Earth Ministry's mission is to engage individuals and congregations in knowing God more fully through deepening relationships with all of God's creation. We believe that through this experience our personal lives and our culture will be transformed. These transformations include simplified living, environmental stewardship, justice for all creation and a world-view which sees creation as a revelation of God. Together these lead to a rediscovery of the vitality of the Christian faith.[24]

But can this statement be substantiated? Does 'knowing God more fully' – in particular, through corporate worship, which is

our theme – really change anything in Christian discipleship, and
if so, precisely what? Some studies on this subject have already
been carried out. Philip Hughes, in an analysis of such surveys,[25]
draws attention to the need for ecological education and asks if
the churches have a part to play in changing people's mindset,
which may lead to new attitudes and more responsible behaviour
towards the environment.[26] The power of the media to raise
awareness and thus develop environmental concern is demonstrated from a number of studies in Australia.[27] As all teachers
know, repetition and frequent exposure are critical factors in
enabling people to learn new things or develop their thinking. In
the USA an increase in the number of articles in *The New York
Times* on the subject of environmental issues did seem to be
accompanied by an increased level of change in behaviour. When
more articles appeared there was more support for environmental spending.

So exposing people to these ideas does make a difference.[28]
Education, attitudes and behaviour in respect to environmental
concern can be measured and are connected. The church at worship is a substantial instrument on a global scale for encouraging
people to learn and thus to change their behaviour. We can be
confident that Christian corporate worship, in whatever way
God and his creation are presented in it, is having an influence on
Christians in their behaviour.

But what exactly changes? And what factors might we see as
significant in producing such change? There is no clear indication
from the studies we have noted that people who merely believed
in God or went to church had greater concern for the environment, or took more specific action about it. One set of results
shows slight evidence that people who did *not* believe in God
were more likely than those who did believe to support environmental organizations.[29] The opposite effect, however, is noted by
others, with committed believers slightly more likely to be
engaged in environmental concerns.[30] The evidence seems to be
confused.

But if it is not the religious beliefs and practices themselves
that produce noticeable environmental concern, what is it?
Hughes argues from this mixed evidence that religious practice
does not directly produce the attitudes, but that it strengthens

what is there already, these previous attitudes being what he calls '"spiritual" orientations', or world-views, which are held by non-religious, as well as religious, people. Underlying attitudes seem to be more influential than any overt religious belief or any other factor, such as age, education, gender and social class.[31] For example, the relationship between concern for the environment and a literal belief in the Bible is not direct, but a certain attitude to the Bible and an attitude to the environment both emerge from that person's underlying world-view. In the USA belief in the inerrancy of the Bible tends to be linked with political conservatism. So those who espouse this general view of the world are, on the one hand, concerned about stewardship at a local level but, on the other hand, are less involved with environmental concerns at a political level.[32]

A person's world-view, therefore, seems to provide a basis for differences in behaviour towards the environment so that different Christian traditions in different social and political contexts produce different outcomes according to these wider attitudes. Strong views about human dominion over creation or a belief that the world is worthy of respect lead, respectively, to lower or higher levels of environmental interest and action.[33] Hughes concludes from his studies that 'the level of environmental concern is not so much a product of personal experience as a product of "ideology" or attitudes'.[34]

This conclusion gives weight to the argument that it is general beliefs about the nature of creation itself that make the difference. Perceptions about the environment – and resulting ecological behaviour – are formed not directly from what may be seen as Christian or Christological beliefs, but from a substratum of convictions about the nature of the world and all its inhabitants, both organic and inorganic. And such convictions may be shared by many others who have environmental concerns. It is this underlying set of convictions that are our concern. In the Christian context, these beliefs about the created world and humanity's relationship to it make up a doctrine of creation.

If what we have argued about the importance and influence of public worship is true, and if such worship leads to changes in behaviour, then it is part of the task of those who prepare and lead services to do so, in the current period of concern about the environment, with an awareness of the doctrine of creation. In the end this matter is about discipleship – how the Christian believer behaves in daily life. Such behaviour has personal and local outcomes but it also implies political involvement and social action.

Inclusion of elements of the doctrine of creation in public worship may change the attitudes of worshippers and strengthen their discipleship, but also, at a more profound level, it may develop new behaviour towards the natural world. We should not continue with a theology and liturgy that is, in Santmire's words, 'seriously deficient'.[35] The global influence of such worship upon Christian people, and then of Christian people on their neighbours, should not be minimised. It is to discuss the position of these neighbours of the church that we now turn for further insight.

The mission opportunity – connecting to unbelievers

In the final section of this chapter we examine a second matter, which is of close interest to the church as it meets regularly for worship. This is the effect of the worship of God in church upon a person who is not a Christian. We will explore what this issue has to do with the presence or absence of creation themes in public worship.

We can begin to tease out this matter by asking the question: What is the person who is not a believer in Christ (or not yet a believer) doing in public worship? I do not mean by this to ask why they are present at the service in the first place. That may be for a variety of reasons, practical or spiritual. One person is there because they are vaguely seeking God, or another may be seriously seeking faith. Another is there because someone has pressed them into coming, and yet another is happily fulfilling a family duty. But when I ask what they are doing, I mean: What is happening to them in the process of the worship? Is there any reality at all that going on with them as they are present? To put it more plainly: Is anything that could be properly described as the worship of the true and living God taking place within them during a Christian service of worship?

Public worship and mission

This question raises the significant issue of the relationship between the church at worship and her mission. The fundamental proposal here is that the presence of creation themes in corporate worship presents a pathway for those who are not yet believers to participate. If such a pathway is provided, it is a significant opportunity for the church at worship to include those who are not yet believers. Neglect of creation themes in public worship therefore seriously reduces that opportunity.

Those present in worship who are not yet ready to confess personal faith in Christ are almost certainly conscious of their own 'createdness', unless they are convinced atheists. Even at a most basic level, by their presence in the service, they are reaching out to honour their Creator. For the worship of such people to have any meaning as they stand among the community of faith at worship, and for them to respond on the basis of their own createdness, requires that the idea and concept of creation be adequately expressed in the content of the service. Human createdness provides a platform for us to develop a theological understanding of worship for those without an obvious Christ-centred faith.

For most traditions of the church, corporate worship is increasingly seen as a vital part of mission. But the church in New Testament times did not seem to expect that unbelievers would be present at their gatherings. In fact, we are told in the book of Acts that people were fearful of joining in.[36] This was in the context of the sudden deaths of Ananias and Sapphira, the couple who tried to deceive the church about a gift of money. The signs and wonders that were done through the apostles created a sense of the power and nearness of God, which led to people being cautious about joining the church. The presence of an unbeliever in their meetings seems to have been an exception.[37]

In the early centuries of the church there was also the possibility of persecution. To be a Christian made you a target, you only went to church if you were a believer or were preparing for baptism. After that, you were allowed to be present at the Eucharist.[38] One outcome of all this was that in the first three centuries the church was quite secretive, and this only changed when the great apologists began to explain more clearly what Christian meetings were about.[39] Before that, people generally became Christians through observing the love, or hearing the witness, of Christians.

The Christendom period led to a mixed situation and people in 'Christian' Europe generally were regarded as believers. It was not until the twentieth century in Europe, as society became more secular, that it was recognised that the public worship of the church was taking place week by week in a society that did not accept the faith of the Christian church. The mentality that viewed public worship as worship on behalf of all the people in the community needed to change. The Roman Catholic Church began to see this in the time of Pope Paul VI, who tentatively recognised the place of the liturgy of the word in evangelization.[40] John Paul II then spoke of his conviction that 'every authentic prayer is prompted by the Holy Spirit, who is mysteriously present in every human heart'.[41] In this way, he includes prayer from persons of unbelief as part of the process of evangelising. There is, however, little in the Roman Church of the idea of witness to unbelievers made by or during the liturgy.[42] Eastern Orthodox theologians, on the other hand, more directly claim that mission and worship go together and have always done so. Debate in the Orthodox Church about the renewal of worship includes the idea of the church at worship in the Eucharist as a place for sharing the gospel,[43] and as the focal point of the mission of the church.[44]

Attention given to music in the Church of England is justified in the most recent report on church music (1992) partly because 'the worship of the church is the foundation of our work and witness in the world, and music can be a powerful means not only for the worshippers but also for reaching out into society'.[45] The authors warn that church worship must not draw too harsh a line between what is sacred and what is secular since that divides what takes place inside the church from what goes on outside it. A 'whole human offering' needs to include more than the obviously religious, particularly when celebrating God's creation.[46]

Many popular books on worship similarly claim that worship needs to be linked to a church's 'vision for evangelism'[47] and be accessible to the unbeliever because the Western church lives in a 'missionary situation'.[48] The advance of missionary activity in the last century has had the effect in many churches of changing the content of services in order to include 'points of contact' for the gospel.[49] Most notable of these changes is the 'seeker service' concept of the 1990s in which the primary motivation for the preparation and conduct of a worship service was the ease with which certain kinds of unbelievers might participate.

All this demonstrates a different attitude in the contemporary church from that of the church over most of its history. We are now in a time when what happens in church services and the mission of the church are seen to be deeply related.

Worship – proclaiming or involving?

Corporate worship as a vehicle for mission may be discussed by looking at the 'worship evangelism' movement in the United States. Sally Morgenthaler argues that as a person is coming towards faith in Christ some knowledge of God's nature is needed before the gospel can be heard and received. This, she maintains, may be enabled by the corporate worship of the church as the preliminary stage in the process of becoming a Christian.[50] A distinction of this kind between a general knowledge of God and knowledge of the gospel illustrates most sharply the basic problem about the non-Christian in a public service. If we regard corporate worship as an aspect of Christian mission, we need to ask in what way such mission functions for that person. This is the question that we raised earlier: What are they doing? Two different answers are possible.

The first answer is that for the person not, or not yet, a Christian believer, public worship functions in a purely educative manner. It is about proclamation of the gospel in order to bring about Christian faith. The unbelieving person present in the service should therefore be regarded as needing to hear the truth of Christ and to respond in penitence and faith. Only after that may that person worship 'in the Spirit' as a true believer. This might be the motivation for creating a 'seeker service', and for including gospel songs and testimony at the evangelistic mission or revival services. On this same basis, in a normal Sunday service, with unbelievers present, a leader should regard it as their duty to include material that makes Christ and his claims clear. This approach will tend to stress the way of salvation through Christ and the need for a response to him. But is this the only thing that the unbeliever is 'doing' in public worship?

The second answer to the question is that the whole content of the service may engage the unbeliever in true worship at the level of their present faith in God. The argument here is that even though a person is not yet fully convinced about Christ it is possible for them to truly worship God at a preliminary level of faith. Such worship, by a person not yet convinced, or not believing in Christ, must then be taking place because they are a created being approaching their Creator, in other words, on the basis of their 'createdness'. This approach fits with the discussion in Chapter 1 about the need for the engagement of the whole person in the process of coming to know things. The worshipping is part of 'coming to know' and is in fact not possible at all without it. The unbeliever in some way believes already in response to the revelation of God's 'eternal power and divine nature' seen through what he has made.[51] On this basis, that response should be enabled more fully during public worship, not hindered or ignored. In many cases it may lead on to the fuller and saving revelation of Christ. What the person is 'doing in the service' is in some manner worshipping the living God, not just hearing about him. All this has clear mission potential for the church. It is a common observation today that people who are regularly present in public church worship often find faith in this context and thus should be the first object of the church's mission.[52]

There is therefore a deep connection between public worship and mission, but it is not merely worship as proclamation, as in an evangelistic service, although the proclaiming of Christ is inevitable in true Christian worship. It is as much about the actual worship by the unbeliever as it is about the presentation of the gospel of Christ. If this connection is to be made effective, then the content of all Christian public worship should take account of the levels of faith that many people have when they come into church. It should enable response from someone beginning or searching as well as the fuller and Christ-centred response of the committed believer. This means that the service must contain sufficient of what may generally be titled 'the doctrine of creation'.

Spirituality and cosmic feeling

This whole matter is very important because of what is happening in contemporary society in relation to what has come to be called its 'spirituality', or, by some, its 'implicit religion'.[53] A large body of evidence in the United States[54] and the United Kingdom[55] shows that a sense of 'createdness' is now being expressed outside the church in terms of people's spiritual awareness. There is definitely a disconnection at this very point between public acts of worship and contemporary society, where people do not generally go to church, but at the same time are not irreligious. The current creative movement of finding ways of 'alternative worship' is an attempt to engage such people at different levels of faith.[56] Draper and Draper comment that these radical departures from the ordinary forms of Christian corporate worship are 'an indictment of the failure of mainstream Christianity to connect with many searchers, both in terms of mission and worship'.[57] In this atmosphere of spiritual searching and awareness of the religious dimensions of life, the church as a whole can learn to connect corporate worship and mission in much more intentional and subtle ways. This subtlety is not about having more deliberate proclamation in public worship, or more 'worship evangelism'. It has to do with the place we give to the doctrine of creation in worship.

The churches, at various times in their history, lost contact with the rhythms and feelings associated with the natural world and thus with the daily routine of the society to which they witnessed. The Eastern Orthodox scholar Alexander Schmemann shows how this happened to the Eastern (Byzantine) Church of the early mediaeval period. He argues that it drifted away from the earliest forms of church worship, which were broad in scope, resounding with 'cosmic thanksgiving' and embracing a vision of the whole of creation and of human history, into a church-orientated and narrow focus on the saving work of God.[58] Then, as the church moved out into the pagan world, it had to deal with a society that seemed to be already in touch with creation through 'a cosmic feeling'. The communities around the churches already had habits and practices in their social, political and economic lives that connected deeply with the rhythm of the natural world.[59] The formal destruction of pagan places and abandonment of their practices did not do away with this feeling. The church needed to fill up the space created by the elimination of pagan worship so it adapted for itself various functions and rituals that related to the agrarian, natural and cosmic environment. These had been connected with the pagan worship before the coming of Christianity and therefore the church had to change its own worship practice in order fully to accomplish its mission. This insight substantiates the fundamental point here. If the act of corporate worship is to be regarded as connected to Christian mission, and is to take proper account of what is taking place in contemporary society, then it will have to change in some way. The change needed is a reconsideration, and new or renewed inclusion, of the doctrine of creation in corporate worship.

Building a better bridge

A further and final question needs to be answered: What exactly are the implications of thinking about Christian corporate worship in terms of mission? One answer is to think more carefully about the content of the songs and hymns selected, particularly in the opening minutes of a service. One survey of preferred wedding hymns shows that creation content is a priority for people who wish to offer worship on such occasions and who hope to enable their guests, possibly unbelieving guests, to do so.[60] The top three choices were: 'All things bright and beautiful', 'Morning has broken' and 'Lord of all hopefulness'. If you trouble to look at these in detail, you will find that none of them has any overt Christological content. They all dwell on creation and God's presence in the world he has made. In opting for these choices for their wedding the couples surveyed are following a deep instinct for what is appropriate in a mixed congregation of believers and unbelievers, as well as expressing their own feeling for celebrating the creation gift of marriage.

For the unbeliever, the introduction of strong Christological themes in public worship changes the direction from honour offered up to the Creator and Sovereign of all to horizontal instruction about the Christian faith and appeal to the unbeliever to respond. This evangelistic dimension is, of course, wholly appropriate and should be suitably encouraged, but recognition of the Creator, and the response of the people as created beings, particularly early on in a service, should not be omitted.

This is the fundamental problem with the bridge-building approach envisaged by Morgenthaler in the 'worship evangelism' concept. She calls for substantive lyrics in such a context, and notes that creation should move on to redemption in worship.[61] However, she is primarily occupied, with the cultural and stylistic elements needed to create a bridge to those coming in from an unchurched background. On this basis, her 'perfect' cross-cultural song is 'Lord, I lift your name on high'. She argues for this song because it has a clear gospel message and because it is personal and passionate.[62] But this song is quite unsuitable for the purposes suggested, particularly in consideration of creation themes as we have been discussing. There is no hint in it of creation or of God as sovereign over the created world, or over human life. So no creation setting is provided for the response of a seeker or unbeliever. The song is clearly addressed to Christ as redeemer, who 'came from heaven to earth to show the way' and invites instant commitment by the singer who is 'so glad you're in my life'. The personal and intimate lines of the song turn any person not yet committed at best into an interested observer, at worst into an embarrassed participant. Such experience for a visitor to a contemporary church is all too common and it is not necessary. There are much better ways of doing what is needed. There are opportunities in many contemporary songs and standard hymns to engage that which already exists in the visitor who may be ready at a primary level to enter into praise.

We have examined a number of reasons, both in the wider context and in the church, why worship in the light of creation is important. There is a pastoral motivation: so that Christians may relate their worship together to the daily lives they live. There is a mission motivation: so that those who come into church services are not excluded by the worship, but drawn in through their own response to discover the creator and redeemer God fully revealed in Jesus Christ.

We have argued that the presence of the doctrine of creation in public worship is a key, perhaps the central key, by which doors are opened to create pathways from worship to the ordinary world of work and the non-Christian society. Praise of the Creator for the natural world is the single most obvious way that such content may be appropriately incorporated into public worship and we will return to this theme. It is thus in the interest of leaders and pastors to incorporate in public worship praise and other fitting responses of awe, recognition and respect from the human creature to the creator. Deliberate development in this direction is urgently needed in many contemporary churches.

But what exactly is the doctrine of creation and what are its dimensions? If churches are deliberately to include creation themes in public worship, we need to describe them in detail. This is the task of the next chapter.

4

The Christian Doctrine of Creation

So, you are sitting down to prepare to lead worship next Sunday
and you want to bear in mind the points we have been making,
and include some more aspects of the doctrine of creation in the
service. What particular things will you need to include? If it is
true that the churches need to give fuller place in public worship
to the doctrine of creation, we need to know what the dimensions
of that doctrine are. Here I draw out ten elements of this aspect of
Christian doctrine, and in doing so I will point out some theological tensions that appear and clarify key issues that are raised
by those tensions.

Significant development in Christian worship in recent
decades has made room for concern about ecology and the environment to influence the content of services. These changes of
language and content can be traced to some extent in the main
denominational service books, which are easy to access.[1] Other
material is less conveniently to hand, but for further illustration
as we proceed I will draw from free-standing liturgical texts in
historical sources and from the survey of recordings of contemporary services noted earlier.[2]

Consideration of the doctrine of creation contains one great difficulty: How do we define its limits? What is to be included and
what excluded? To think of God and his creation is, in fact, to
think of everything that exists and thus of all subjects in theology.
For example, it is not possible to explore the Christian theology of
creation without considering how and why the Son of God
became a man within that creation. Nor is it possible to ignore the
doctrine of the Holy Spirit since the Spirit is the one who gives life
to all things and moves upon creation to bring the presence of

God near. These have a direct bearing on our view of God as creator and on the way we see the relationship with creation of both God and humanity. Nevertheless, we need to set some limits to the discussion. So in the following outline of the doctrine of creation we discuss humanity, the incarnation of Christ and the place of the Spirit only in relation to their connection with the created world.

The Christian doctrine of creation may therefore be defined in a general way as: *Christian teaching about the creator God and the created order and the manner of God's relationship as creator to that creation.* Immediately we can see that there are two distinct sides to this subject:

- the creator.
- that which is created.

As we consider the ten elements of the doctrine of creation, we will look at them from both these aspects.

1. God as the unaided and unconstrained creator of all things

Christian doctrine affirms that God created the universe by his own free decision without any prior existing force or external influence acting upon him. If there were such a force or influence, then God would not be entirely free of constraints. God would not be truly God if there were something outside himself that made him act the way he did, or stopped him doing what he chose to do. In Christian doctrine, therefore, God is, and always was, free and unconstrained in the work of creation. The language of worship reflects this conviction.

One way that God's freedom in creating is expressed is by the concept of *creatio ex nihilo*, 'creation out of nothing'. Most branches of the church have accepted that God created out of nothing, even though the expression 'out of nothing' does not appear exactly in the Bible. The beginning of the book of Genesis reads, 'In the beginning when God created the heavens and the earth . . .',[3] but neither the Hebrew of this verse nor the Greek translation of it in the Septuagint explicitly supports the idea of there being nothing at all before that moment of creation. Some theologians in both ancient and recent times have therefore felt free to suggest that God 'made' or 'formed' the universe out of pre-existing matter. However, the concept of 'the beginning' in both the Old and New Testaments implies a sudden and totally new universe, before which there was nothing but God.[4]

In Jewish writings in the time following the formation of the Old Testament, we find that God 'made the world out of things that had no existence', that he 'called from the beginning of the world that which did not yet exist' and that he commanded 'that visible things should come down from invisible'.[5] The writer of the New Testament book of Hebrews lived with this kind of thinking and so he is able to say, 'what is seen was made from things that are not visible'.[6] This statement does not in so many words assert *creatio ex nihilo*, but it does affirm that the Creator had nothing visible to the senses with which to work his creation of the world. The expression 'all things' in the New Testament, which includes both the visible earthly world and the invisible heavenly world according to Colossians 1.16, suggests that nothing exists apart from what God has created.[7]

The alternatives to the concept of 'creation out of nothing' have serious consequences for the church and its doctrine. They affect many of the key points we discuss below and some features today in Christian public worship. One such problem is the likelihood of confusing the being of God with creation, which we consider under the concept of God's transcendence. The idea that God created out of some pre-existent matter owes more to ancient Hindu thought, and Greek ideas of the pre-Christian era, than to Hebrew thought as represented by the Old Testament. It has led more than one Christian thinker into the error of dualism: the idea that God and spiritual things are good and that matter and physical things are in some way evil.[8]

But for the biblical writers, there is nothing else which God has to take account of in his creative work, nothing that restricts him or influences him in any way. The writers of the Old Testament make this clear in a number of ways. So, for example, the God of Israel created the sun, moon and stars. They were not there before. They are not 'gods', or powers with an existence of their own, to be feared or worshipped. They are described as not having inherent powers, but as mere calendars and clocks to organise time, which God has created, and to help give rhythm to human life.[9] The prophets of Israel worked on the assumption that there is no merely secular part of life that is outside God's interest or rule. He created it all, and therefore trouble and joy, life and death, worship and family, field and temple, all belong to God. There is no evil force of equal power to God that restricts him. There is no 'secular' realm over which he has no rule. It is all 'holy, holy, holy'.

As we might expect, God's creative work seen in this way occurs as a regular defining sentence in almost all traditional and current liturgy and certainly in all carefully prepared written liturgy. Based on biblical precedent, the church has made the first sentence of every creed the confession of faith in God as creator, or maker, of all things. God is 'creator of heaven and earth', 'maker of heaven and earth, of all things visible and invisible'[10] or 'of all that is, seen and unseen'.[11] The line also has appeared for generations in many places in service books of nonconformist Churches, so that God is declared to be 'creator of all things'[12] and 'God the Father who made the world'.[13] In some liturgies the words specifically state creation out of nothing. In the Orthodox liturgy in the Order for the Lord's Prayer before Communion the priest prays: 'We thank you, King invisible, who by your boundless power created all things, in the abundance of your mercy bringing them into being out of nothing.'[14]

In the seventeenth-century *Book of Common Prayer*, and therefore in all subsequent Anglican liturgies for Morning Prayer, the psalmody of the opening part of the service includes substantial emphasis on God as creator and Lord of the created order. Other parts of these liturgies develop the theme. Consistent use of these traditional forms presents a strong vision of God as creator. The clarity and consistency of this first belief has been regularly expressed in Christian liturgy and is not questioned within any worship tradition.

We have explored the most basic feature of the Christian doctrine of creation: God alone as creator of all things, unaided and without constraint, without the need for pre-existent material or limits imposed by it. Because of its long and largely secure tradition in

Christian doctrine, we should expect to find content expressing this feature represented regularly in services. But is this so? Are such statements present in all churches and all services? This is one of the key questions that we have set out to discover.

2. God as transcendent

For God to be transcendent means that he is above and beyond and separate in his essential being from the world he has made. It does not mean that he is indifferent, uninvolved, detached and uninterested in his creation. It means that he is not to be confused in his essential being with his creation. God and creation are two separate things. The biblical witness to God's transcendence, understood in this way, is overwhelming and it has always been central to the Christian doctrine of God. In the Old Testament God is described as one who 'sits in the heavens', who has set his glory 'above the heavens' and as one who is 'over all he has made'.[15] He is depicted as king of all creation, ruler of the nations and judge of the world.[16]

A significant point of tension is raised here because the transcendent God needs also to be related to, and present in, his creation. It is important for us to examine this problem since this theological tension is expressed in many radical and new ecological liturgies, and we will look at examples in Chapter 5. Irenaeus, a bishop of Lyons in the second century, had a literary battle with the Gnostic teachers of his day.[17] In these arguments, which set the tone for all subsequent Christian discussion of the nature of God, a clear distinction is set between the transcendent God and Father of Jesus Christ and all other created things.[18] The same argument is being conducted today, not only with new 'gnostic' theologies, but also within the Christian tradition between those who hold to the concept of God's transcendence and those who want to emphasise the presence of God in the created world.

One recent writer, Paul Brockelman, sees the divine presence actively working in the natural world so that this presence can be described as 'a gigantic breath – a great cry – which we call God'. He argues that God's transcendence is then found in the human response of wonder at the mystery of life itself. The experience of amazement at the power of anything and all things to exist at all becomes the transcendent. Put into terms generally understood, the experience of transcendence itself becomes God.[19] We can see how in this scheme the nature and being of God is confused with the nature and being of created things in their variety. The transcendent God is no longer a divine being who stands behind and beyond the being of all things that exist because he has no separate identity from them. The God who is transcendent, in that he is personal, free, sovereign and not dependent on the world he has made, has disappeared in favour of a God whose transcendence is inevitably linked to the matter of the universe: he is the 'world soul'.

Another version of this idea puts it in reverse. God as 'world soul' becomes the world as the 'body of God'.[20] The work of Sallie McFague can represent this thinking. Her writing takes serious account of the 'common creation story', by which she means the scientifically demonstrated account of the origins and evolutionary progress of the universe. She is seeking a renewed organic or connected view of the world and its relationship to God. She wants to hold transcendence (separateness) and immanence (closeness) in tension, and in doing so to 'magnify God's transcendence'.[21] However, what she means by 'transcendence' is very different from the traditional understanding of a transcendent God. Transcendence is 'a form of meditation' that we are able to practise as we think of the world as 'the body of God'. Something beyond all the particular items of the world is found in the many diverse things that exist and so we perceive the transcendence of God in the variety and difference between them. The result of this is that 'God is many, not one, for the body of God is not one body (except as a universe) but the infinite number of bodies . . . that are the universe'.[22]

There are a number of significant problems with this concept, but it is being reflected in some of the contemporary liturgies that we will look at in Chapter 5. The concept of world soul, or body of God, confuses the nature of the uncreated God and the nature of created things. If God is the sole creator, he must be a different kind of being from every other thing that exists. If we identify the nature of God as the same in essence as the nature of the world he has created, we end with pantheism: that everything is God. The transcendence of God in any traditional sense then vanishes, as also does God's free constitution of the world in its own being.

Of course, we still have to answer the difficult question about the way that a transcendent God continues to relate to his created universe and how he is active within it. Those who write of 'world soul' or the 'body of God' have made serious attempts to do so, but have lost sight of the transcendent God in the process. The manner of God's relationship to, and presence in, the created world is to be sustained in a very different way (see pp. 113).[23]

The concept of the transcendence of God holds together every other aspect of Christian theology. It is therefore very important for us to sustain it in public worship, but there are signs that the church at worship may be losing sight of this important understanding of God's nature. The doctrine of God as transcendent is reflected in all the main liturgical traditions and has been the underlying atmosphere of them. In particular, Eastern Orthodox liturgies convey a vision of the eternal God beyond the universe so that the wonder of the incarnation of the Word may be more clearly displayed.[24]

A few examples will give us a flavour of this worship. In one prayer early in the *Divine Liturgy* God is viewed as above the world in all respects:

> Lord God, whose might is beyond compare and whose glory is beyond understanding, whose mercy is without measure, and whose love for man is beyond all telling, look upon us and upon this holy house . . .
>
> (Prayer of the First Antiphon)[25]

In this passage God's title is expanded with phrases emphasising his uniqueness. The triple use of the term 'beyond' creates the vision of a God not only greater in being, but above and separate from the worshippers who ask for him to 'look upon' them from his heights.

Titles used for God in the Orthodox liturgy have the effect of raising a vision of the transcendent God. In various places we find phrases such as,

Holy God, Holy Strong, Holy Immortal . . . Lord our God dwelling on high and beholding things below . . . O King of Glory . . . You alone, Lord our God, are Ruler over all things, in heaven and on earth . . . Lord of the Seraphim and King of Israel, the only Holy One . . . King invisible.

Many passages in the liturgy take similar paths of thought.

> You are God, ineffable, incomprehensible, invisible, inconceivable, ever existing, eternally the same; you and your only-begotten Son and your Holy Spirit. You brought us out of non-existence into being . . .
>
> (The Holy Oblation)[26]

During the pre-communion prayer the priest says,

> We thank you, King invisible, who by your boundless power created all things, in the abundance of your mercy bringing them into being out of nothing. Do you yourself, Master, look down from heaven . . .
>
> (*The Preparation for Holy Communion*)[27]

These sentences not only express clarity on 'creation out of nothing', as we have previously discussed, but they emphasise the being of God as utterly other than that which he created. This theology is in deliberate contrast to any view that regards the world as an emanation from God, or as identified with him, and this is consistent with the general history of Christian thinking.[28]

In other traditional liturgies the same emphasis is found, although not in such expansive phrases. In the Te Deum and Benedicite a vision of heavenly worship is given, with angels surrounding the person of God in his holiness and transcendence. The Sanctus, used in some form in all the main denominational liturgies, also conveys a conviction of the utter transcendence of God:

> Holy, holy, holy Lord, God of power and might,
> heaven and earth are full of your glory.
> Hosanna in the highest.

So the second aspect of the Christian doctrine of creation that we may expect to find in public worship is content showing God as transcendent. This has been so for the whole of Christian history. But new questions are now being asked about the relationship of God to the world and his presence in the world, particularly in the light of ecological awareness.

3. God as the sustainer and provider

Here we discuss one aspect of a broader doctrine: the concept of the providence of God, *creatio continua*, his continuing or ongoing work with his creation. The doctrine of God's providence is commonly divided into two parts. The first part is about the way that God preserves or sustains his creation. The second is about God's government in leading forward his purposes. Since our concern is the doctrine of creation and God's relationship with the natural order, we are looking at the first of these two aspects: providence as God's continuing creative work in preserving the universe by his power and activity and making natural provision for the sustained life of his creatures.

The biblical basis for this doctrine needs little emphasis. In Genesis 1 God commands that all plants and fruit should be food for humankind and for animals,[29] and in the Old Testament God promises blessing on the land he gives so that it produces sustenance for his people.[30] Israel, in her worship, repeatedly expresses confidence in the provision of God for human beings and animals. He provides for hunger and thirst, and for personal security, summed up in the great description of God's provision for all living things in Psalm 104 in which the worshipper sings in verse 13, 'The earth is satisfied with the fruit of your work.' God is to be worshipped for his goodness, expressed repeatedly as a motive for worship: 'Praise the LORD, for he is good.' His generosity, through good gifts, surrounds his people in the world he has made.

The central statement of this doctrine in the New Testament must be the Lord's Prayer request to 'give daily bread'. The knowledge of God's good natural gifts underlies the apostle's instruction that food is to be received with thanksgiving,[31] as well as being the grounds for generosity to the poor.[32] A vision of God as sustainer and provider for the whole world lies beneath all Scripture and all Christian teaching.

The creating power of God is further seen as he provides for, cherishes, instils new vigour and bestows power on his creatures so they may continue to exist and live in his world. Gunton stresses that in Christian doctrine creation is understood as the work of the Son and Spirit as well as of the Father. Therefore Christians also see the conserving and preserving of the natural order, along with saving providence and redemption, as the work of God as Trinity.[33] The doctrine of providence has a Trinitarian structure. God engages with, is present in and sustains the world he has created in his being as Father, Son and Spirit. The consequence of his continual sustaining and provision is the total dependence of all creation on God. These first three features that we have considered hang together and are interlocked. The first act of creation now requires continual generous provision.

Acknowledging God's provision for and sustaining of the universe in this way is in evidence in the worship of the early church. In the *Didache*, a first-century document that outlines the content of one form of early public worship, we find

> You, Almighty Master, created all things for Your name's sake, and gave food and drink to men for enjoyment, so that they might render thanks to You.[34]

Clement of Rome exhorts the Corinthian church in the late first century to praise God for the natural gifts of life in whatever state they find themselves as created beings:

> Let us consider . . . He who made us and fashioned us, having prepared His bountiful gifts for us before we were born, introduced us into His world. Since, therefore, we receive all these things from Him, we ought for everything to give Him thanks; to whom be glory for ever and ever. Amen.
>
> (*Clement*, The First Epistle of Clement)[35]

It is not necessary to rehearse this theme throughout the history of Christian liturgy since its inclusion in public worship has been so widespread. Whatever else public worship might include or exclude, it has rarely omitted acknowledgement of God's providence and gifts of creation. It should be expected to appear significantly in any form of Christian public worship.

4. God present in creation

The fourth feature of the doctrine of creation is that God is present in his creation through the activity of the Holy Spirit. Genesis 1:2, which speaks of the 'spirit of God' moving over the face of the waters, is given various translations in different versions of the Bible. Often possible alternatives are shown in a footnote. So the Good News Bible translates these words as 'the power of God was moving over the waters', and then in a footnote helpfully offers '*or* the spirit of God; *or* a wind from God; *or* an awesome wind'. All of these are possible translations, but the church has always interpreted this verse as an indication in the Old Testament of the doctrine of the Holy Spirit. God here is present and active within his creation and this presence and power is made possible by the Spirit.

If the Spirit was present in the very act of creation of the universe, then this implies the Spirit's continuing presence. The Old Testament makes the same 'spirit' of God the source of natural gifts of craftsmanship when design and construction skills are needed to create the place of worship.[36] The psalmist prays in the knowledge of God's presence in every place and time and condition of human experience, and asks, 'Where can I go from your spirit, or where can I flee from your presence?'[37]

The Christian doctrine of the Spirit therefore offers a solution to the problem about the confusion of the being of world and the being of God that we discussed earlier. The Spirit enables Christian theology to hold a view of the universe as a reality independent from the transcendent God, but at the same time of God as present and working with and upon the matter of the world. This is the concept of the 'immanence' of God.

God is not just present in the universe by the Spirit, however, he also sustains it by his presence. When the apostle Paul was in Athens, he used a line of poetry, attributed by scholars to

Epimenides of Crete, 'In him we live and move and have our being', in order to build a bridge for his gospel preaching. He was trading on the universal sense that people have – 'as even some of your own poets have said' – that God is everywhere and that in particular his human creation only exists because he is sustaining their existence.[38]

At the end of the first two centuries, Iranaeus summed up Christian thinking about how God relates to his creation with the image, current in the second century, of the 'two hands of God'. In arguing against false views he used words from the psalms to show that the material world, and in particular humankind, are 'moulded by his hands, that is the Son and the Spirit'.[39] He develops this concept, stating that it was the 'Word and Wisdom, the Son and the Spirit, through whom and in whom he made everything'.[40] The Holy Spirit, therefore, as well as the Son, is the one 'by whom all things were made', always present with humanity from the very beginning in all the different periods of God's activity in the world.[41]

Such a view of the Spirit present in all creation is not controversial and is expressed in most standard liturgies. It is, however, an important doctrine for us to uphold in both theology and public worship because, as we have seen, it enables God's presence without confusion of his nature with the nature of the world. One of Gunton's distinctives of the Christian doctrine of creation is the recognition of creation as a work of God in his three persons.[42] We need to maintain the separate identity and integrity of the whole created world and the actual presence of God in his world, without confusing the two. This aspect of the doctrine of creation, the presence of the Sprit in creation, is the simplest way of doing so.

When we turn to examine the liturgies of the church, we find that in many places assertions are made about the presence of God in creation, either in particular reference to the Holy Spirit, or to God the creator active in his creation. The Nicene Creed declares faith in 'the Holy Spirit, the Lord and giver of life'. The Sanctus, taken from Isaiah 6, an important liturgical text appearing in all standard liturgies from the earliest Christian churches, states that 'heaven and earth are full of your glory'.[43] The 'glory' here is best understood in the Old Testament sense of the presence of God shining out in a visible way so that within and behind the created things of heaven and earth the presence of God can be perceived.

The subtlety needed to hold together the immanence of God without confusing the being of God and the world can be seen in devotional as well as liturgical texts. For example, part of the fourth-century *Hymn Against Bar-Daisan* includes the lines,

> As the water surrounds the fish and feels it,
> So also do all natures feel God.
> He is diffused through the air,
> And with thy breath enters into thy midst.
> He is mingled with the light,
> And enters, when thou seest, into thy eyes.
> He is mingled with thy spirit,
> And examines thee from within, as to what thou art,
> In thy soul He dwells
> And nothing which is in thy heart is hid from him.
>
> (*Ephrem the Syrian* [306–73])

Here Ephrem is trying to express the understanding that God is present to and with everything, that we cannot distance God from his creation. He is also careful, however, to maintain an orthodox theology of God as transcendent – different from his creation. There is a very fine line between these expressions of the relation of God to matter and what might be read as pantheism. In this hymn God, like the water that surrounds the fish, surrounds all created beings, but is not to be identified with them. He enters with human breath and mingles with the light, but he is not actually the breath, or the light. Ephrem has constructed his hymn with great care to avoid confusion of the being of light or of breath with the being of God. This is a worthy meditation on the presence of God in creation.

These few texts show how ancient material, traditional liturgies and prayers have included the doctrine of the immanence of God in his creation. In Chapter 5 we discuss other more recent examples, which show an inclination to unite the being of the world and the being of God. This is one area where there appears to be significant shift in liturgical practice in the light of current ecological concerns. It is the most significant tension represented by the matter we are discussing.

5. Creation, the Son and the incarnation

The fifth feature is how God is related to creation in the person of God the Son and in his incarnation. The New Testament writers' testimony to Christ as the one through whom the world was created is part of their declaration of his deity.[45] Tertullian in the second century seems to have been the first to have used the image of the 'two hands' of God, pointing out that the psalmist says, 'The heavens are the work of your hands.'[46] So he says that Christ the Word 'is the Lord's right hand, indeed his two hands, by which he worked and constructed the universe'.[47] Irenaeus developed this concept in a Trinitarian direction so that the Word, as one of the two hands of God, is 'the creator of the world'.[48]

There is very little in the older liturgies or worship material that shows the presence of the humanity of Christ. There are two reasons for this. The first is that the subject of creation largely appears in these liturgies as material drawn from the Old Testament. There is therefore much about God creating and sustaining the world but no reference to Christ. The whole of the beginning of Morning Prayer in *The Book of Common Prayer* is of this kind. The same can be said for nonconformist material offered for Sunday worship. This is not surprising since the intention was to follow a theological structure in worship that begins with God and creation and later moves to the person of Christ and salvation.

The second reason is that the creeds and Eucharistic prayers of Christian worship rightly dwell on the salvation accomplished in Christ. Statements about the creation and sustaining of the world are therefore attached to the action of the Father, to God in a general sense, not to Christ as the agent of that creation.

There are a few exceptions in traditional material. The Nicene Creed has, in the section about Christ, the words, 'Being of one substance with the Father, by whom all things were made.' And the Roman Catholic Tridentine Mass, in the Gospel reading after Communion, uses John 1, so the liturgy includes the words spoken of the divine Word, 'All things were made by him and without him was made nothing that was made.' In the Orthodox liturgy, Christ is given the titles 'King of all things' and 'Master of creation'.[49] These examples show that the doctrine of Christ as the one through whom the world was made and in whom it is sustained has not been entirely omitted in standard liturgies.

In Christian theology the relationship of God to the material world is expressed and enabled by the incarnation of the Son. But there is a lack of attention to this idea in liturgical use. Theologians have tended in the past to discuss the person of Christ in relation to God's saving work and thus to omit 'cosmic christology'.[50] This has been particularly true of the Reformed tradition in which the incarnation is discussed only in terms of the need of sinful humanity for a mediator and saviour. For example, Calvin says: 'The only end which the Scripture uniformly assigns to the Son of God voluntarily assuming our nature and even receiving it as a command from the Father, is, that he might propitiate the Father to us by becoming a victim.'[51] The issue, however, is important and cannot be swept aside in favour of an emphasis on the redeeming work of Christ. The answer to thinking of God as distant from his creation is a robust theology of the incarnation.

The whole solution to the question of God's relationship to the world, however, is to be found not only in the incarnation of Christ and the presence of the Spirit in creation, but in the nature of God as Trinity. God relates to the material created world not just as its creator and sustainer, but as the one who is connected directly with it through incarnation. He has taken up into himself the material world he created, but at the same time he remains free as truly God.

The incarnation as an aspect of the doctrine of creation is not easily illustrated from the text of traditional liturgies. It appears obliquely when Christian worship takes up and uses a variety of material things. It is presented visibly in the Eucharist, where the incarnation is expressed by the action and the accompanying thanksgiving for Christ 'the living bread that came down from heaven'.[52] When, however, we examine words spoken rather than action, we find very few Christological references that specifically associate the incarnation with creation as a whole.

The Te Deum includes the phrase 'thou didst not abhor the virgin's womb', which shows that the physicality of human conception and birth are not contrary to the nature of God. The Apostles' Creed describes in simple words the progress of Christ: 'conceived . . . born . . . suffered . . . crucified, dead and buried . . . rose again'. You can read these words only in the light of his redeeming work. Or you might be able to see in them a broader concept – God in Christ identifying with the material world and human experience. In whatever way they are read the words show that the material condition of the incarnate Christ is not contrary to the nature of God, but that he chooses to relate to the material world in the person of the incarnate Son.

The longer Nicene Creed, however, specifies an emphasis on the saving purpose of the incarnation. In the opening phrase of the Christological passage, Christ came: 'for us men and for our salvation'. The creed then follows with the same stress on the physicality of the process of incarnation. The Orthodox liturgy similarly notes only the saving work of Christ. The Son and Word of God: 'accepted for our salvation to take flesh from the holy Mother of God and Ever-Virgin Mary and without change became man'.[53]

The overall picture in the older liturgies is that the incarnation, though expressed in very physical terms and including the general human experiences of life, is viewed as being for salvation for the human race rather than as connected with the created order as a whole. In these liturgies, the emphasis falls on celebration and rehearsal of the salvation that is in Christ. We find nothing to indicate that the incarnation enables a new dimension of the relationship of God to the created order, nor that it has in any way affected creation in the saving purposes being worked out in Christ. If we look for indications that God in Christ enters the experience of human weakness and suffering, we find that this is implicit in the creeds and other state-ments about the incarnation, but that in none of the traditional liturgies is it made explicit. These are matters that are beginning to be noted in the theological world, but they are not yet generally expressed in public worship. Nevertheless, the incarnation of Christ is vital to a broad view of the doctrine of creation.

6. The goodness of created things

The sixth factor is the goodness and value of all things created. In Chapter 4 we noted the danger of people despising the works of God in his physical creation in favour of more 'spiritual' things. This is the error of dualism and it appears regularly, in various forms, in contemporary Christian worship. The theological debates about the nature of God in the first two centuries concluded with the Nicene Creed's affirmation of God as 'maker of heaven and earth, of all that is seen and unseen'. Spiritual and material, heavenly and earthly, all are valued as created by God. The inherent goodness of creation is because it is set free and has value in its own right. It stands on its own two feet, as it were, not separated from God, but in 'relative independence' of its sovereign creator.[54] Gunton coins the term *Selbständigkeit* for this idea; the whole created order standing before its maker in its own separate being,[55] dependent on him for its existence and declared 'very good' for what it is.[56]

God's goodness, together with the goodness of his created world, has been commonly reflected in all standard Christian liturgies. In *The Book of Common Prayer* the opening words in the services of Morning and Evening Prayer include a reference to God's 'infinite goodness and mercy'. Its psalms include the refrain 'the Lord is good', and its whole spirit is of thanks for the goodness of God. Nonconformist liturgies are also rich in this respect, so in the Baptist Union's *Orders and Prayers for Church Worship*, thanks are offered for, 'the manifold enjoyments of our daily life, and for every blessing of body and soul', and for, 'the wonderful gift of life, with all its joys and responsibilities, its experiences and opportunities'.[57]

In the Reformed tradition, the relationship of public worship to daily work, family and community life also appears, as in the following prayer:

> To labour diligently and cheerfully in our several callings
> When on the morrow we return to our daily life and labour.
> By Thy mercy that we may present our bodies as living sacrifices,
> As faithful servants doing our work as in your sight.
>
> (A Manual for Ministers)[58]

This mood of celebrating the goodness of creation is strong in older liturgies. In these and many other similar statements and prayers the church for many centuries has upheld the goodness and value of the created order.

Christian thinking in general, however, and Protestant thought in particular, because of an emphasis on human sinfulness and the Fall, has sometimes moved in the direction of devaluing human nature and creation.[59] Worshippers acknowledge that we live in 'the darkness of this world' in the 'toils, anxieties and distractions of another week' and the 'harsh demands of the world'.[60] The world is a 'valley of tears' and a 'place of exile'.[61] *The Book of Common Prayer*, however, avoids such terminology entirely.

Thus the manner in which the subject of the goodness of creation is handled varies in the older liturgies and it is possible to discern emphases that reflect either a positive or a negative view of the created order. The same is true of contemporary worship.

7. The human and non-human creation

The relationship of the human to the non-human creation begins with God's mandate to human beings in Genesis 1:28. Here Adam and Eve are blessed and are told 'to multiply, and fill the earth and subdue it; and have dominion over . . . every living thing' and are given all vegetation to use as food. This thought also occurs in Psalm 8, where human beings are placed 'over the works of your hands'.[62] Humanity is thus the centre of creation, placed to rule and to use what God has made. Until comparatively recently there was little challenge to this interpretation of these ideas, which seemed to imply total domination of the created order. The conclusion was drawn that human domination and exploitation of the earth's resources was the only biblical and thus the Christian position. The World Council of Churches, for example, could state in 1961 that 'the Christian should welcome the scientific discoveries as new steps in man's dominion of nature'.[63]

We have already seen that the relationship of the human to the non-human creation understood as 'dominance' is held to be the underlying cause of the damage that Western capitalism has done to the environment since the industrial revolution.[64] Sallie McFague abandons ideas of dominion in favour of a 'more Christian' ecological model of relating to the natural world that she sees emerging in postmodern understandings of reality.[65] She argues that the truly Christian way to think about nature is as 'more like,' not as 'unlike' ourselves; the 'arrogant eye', she says, needs to be replaced by the 'loving eye'. Such a change leads to a spirituality of nature, sensitivity to the natural world that sees the world as subject and is the opposite of domination.[66]

However, we do not have to abandon the biblical understanding of dominion entirely simply because the concept has been wrongly interpreted and applied. More moderate voices have emerged seeking a balanced approach to the relationship of human to non-human creation. It is possible to think of the relationship of humanity to creation as more complex. Mastery over nature, harmony with nature and threat from nature are all possible responses in any human situation.[67] Human mastery or dominion over nature is not a ruthless rule and exploitation but rather 'a calling to be and act in such a way as to enable the created order to be itself as a response of praise to its maker'.[68] In other words, the outcome of the command to 'fill the earth and subdue it' need not be consumerist and destructive, but a way of living in which dominion includes elements of subjugation and harmony.

It is almost impossible to find in any older liturgical material any examples of prayer or other liturgical practice to illustrate this theology. All traditions consistently emphasise the provision of God, as we have already shown. The productivity of the earth and natural world, where it is included at all in liturgical texts, is mentioned with reference to the supply of human need and for the use of humankind. Consequently, rather than showing awareness of the value of the things in themselves, or a harmony of human relationship with them, the mastery aspect is emphasised. In worship gifts of creation are spoken of as for human benefit, without hint that humanity needs to preserve or work in harmony with natural things.

There is, however, one clear place where in older liturgical prayer a different relationship to the non-human creation is implied. In the Litany, or General Supplication, in *The Book of Common Prayer*, threat from nature is included. The worshipper acknowledges that without God's protection, disaster from weather or plague is possible. Prayer can be offered about rain and waters, scarcity and dearth, great sickness and mortality, plague and grievous sickness, all of which reflect a fearful relationship to the natural world about us.

However, this is one area of worship practice that has begun to change in our time, as it should in response to the environmental challenge. Such change is also one significant way of responding to criticism of the church's 'dominion theology'. In the long term it is the most important of any changes that can be made in Christian public worship.

8. The spoiling of creation by sin

As I write, the world is horrified because in the last few days large areas of Burma have been swept away by a cyclone and the Sichuan province of China has been struck by a devastating earthquake, both with enormous loss of life. How can anyone go to church next Sunday and celebrate the beauty and joy of God's creation? It seems mad to sing, 'All things bright and beautiful' or, 'All creation worships you' in such a context. Developing creation themes in worship raises the criticism that a merely rosy view of the natural world is presented, a view that owes more to the romantic poets than to Christianity. Worship about, or in the setting of, a beautiful creation, can be mere escapism from the reality of a world where bad events happen all the time. Or it can be a way of avoiding the stressful world we live in to have a religion without any serious moral or theological demands.[69] The mid-twentieth-century revival of Celtic worship and spirituality, with its creation emphasis, has been criticised for exactly this reason.[70]

There is some resistance to introducing creation themes in liturgy because they resonate too much with pre-Christian pagan practices.[71] The Old Testament worshippers, however, combine joy in creation with submission to God in a natural world that is often a threat. The prophet Joel calls Israel to mourning and repentance, and he does so by linking the unfaithfulness of the people to the destructive forces that have been let loose in the natural environment. The judgements of God that Joel describes are connected to what we would call natural disasters, which have come as a result of the nation forsaking God.[72] So Joel's call to renewed worship is first to penitence for the sins that have resulted in these disasters.[73] The consequent blessing after repentance is visualised in very natural terms.[74]

Christian theology is more cautious than Joel's in that it does not link disaster directly with the judgement of God. But Joel's main idea – that such disaster needs to result in corporate humbling and return to God in worship – is certainly right. The New Testament fully agrees about the link between human behaviour and the darkness of the natural world. Creation, both human and non-human, is groaning and under stress because of suffering and decay and is awaiting final release.[75] Creation is not to be seen merely in terms of wonder, thankfulness and joy. Its abuse by humankind and the decay to which it is subjected are to be reasons for penitence and serious consideration in public worship.

Apart from contemporary liturgical material, it is difficult to find any evidence of such matters in the traditional or standard material. There is repeated reference to individual sin and reconciliation between persons, but there is nothing about the damage that this has brought on the non-human world. Such ideas are a very recent development.

9. The restoration of creation

The ninth factor is the restoration of creation through Christ and the Spirit. What we believe about the final restoration of the universe largely depends upon our understanding of the Fall and the extent to which human sin has affected the non-human creation. The range of views can be summarised in three ways. First, the Fall may be seen as a sudden descent from a state of original perfection. In this view the need of the world after the Fall is for full 'restoration' to that perfection that is brought about by Christ in his incarnation, death and resurrection in saving

humanity from sin. Origen and Augustine tend to this view.[76]
Second, the Fall may be seen as a 'brief impediment', or a falter-
ing step on the way to the ultimate perfection of all things. This
approach also takes secular forms, as in the evolutionary ideas of
Hegel and Darwin.

Third, there is the 'transformative' view.[77] In this thinking the
act of creation is a beginning, but not an end. Creation is good
and beautiful and is given life by the Spirit, but it is not perfect,
and so the Spirit has been at work from the beginning to bring it
to perfection. In the fourth century Basil of Caesarea called the
Holy Spirit the 'perfecter' of the world and said, 'He perfects all
other things and himself lacks nothing.'[78] Movement towards
God's perfection, enabled and ordered by the Spirit, is therefore
in the nature of the world as originally created, not as a remedy
for the Fall. From the start, creation had a further destination in
God's plan, a 'completion' to which all things are moving. The
end in view is greater than the beginning and was always to have
been so.

The restoration that is needed is therefore the transforming of
the world that God created as well as the saving of sinful human
beings, who have missed the original pathway towards perfection and damaged the whole creation as a result. The effect of this
understanding is that the moral dimension of human sinfulness
takes its place alongside the original need for movement towards
completion. Sinful human beings are not the only things in the
world that need changing: everything in the universe needs to be
changed. This will be accomplished through Christ and this is
God's great purpose for his whole creation.

The material available in the standard liturgies on the theme of
the restoration of creation is limited. The focus in all texts is on
the future coming of Christ, as in the phrase from the New
Testament Eucharist, 'until he comes'.[79] In the classical creeds the
emphasis is on the resurrection of the human body, so 'we look
for the resurrection from the dead and the life of the world to
come'. Belief in a future with God is declared in other ways too,
as in the appeal, 'and bring us to eternal life', which concludes
many prayers. However, the transformation of creation is not
made clear in such phrases. They simply show that there will be
a consummation of earthly life and that this is to be revealed

when Jesus comes again. Altogether, there is meagre evidence for this particular feature of the doctrine of creation. The liturgies indicate that there will be a restoration, but its dimensions are largely conceived in terms of human resurrection. The wider creation receives no such promise.

10. The goal of creation

The final feature of the doctrine of creation is the ultimate goal of creation. Two basic views are possible. In one there is a place for the present physical universe in a continuing or restored form. In the other the attention is on the heavenly or spiritual future, which implies an ending of the physical universe or its transformation into something entirely different. If, however, the church is encouraged to see its destiny entirely in other-worldly terms in heaven, and if this world and all in it is to be finally destroyed, the primary task is spiritual preparation for that world. In this scheme there is little motivation for improving the environment for future generations, who will also be taken out of it to heaven at the end. This is the view that has been dominant in Christian history.

By contrast, if you see a future for the present creation in a newly restored heaven and earth, then there is great motivation for doing something about its present state. This view has been depicted in very material terms. Irenaeus regards the final state of humankind as physical and bodily resurrection in an earthly kingdom in which God will 're-organise the mystery of the glory of [His] sons'. He specifically denies the view that this existence will be in 'a super-celestial place'.[80] The material is not to be superseded by the merely spiritual, but the world we know has eternal value and will have a place in God's restored universe.

Support for this view is found from contemporary New Testament scholars.[81] The early Christian hope does not seem to be simply about 'going to heaven when we die', but for 'a new heaven and new earth'. The doctrine of the resurrection of the body points in this direction. Christians are to look for 'a massive act of new creation'.[82] The conclusion of all this is therefore that the world is good, but not complete and God will renew it. So everyone should work towards its renewal because God has wonderful final plans for it

The traditional liturgies have tended to emphasise movement from this world to an eternal heavenly world at the end of life. They are thus open to the criticism of being world-denying rather than world-affirming. Sentences such as 'preserve my soul for everlasting life', 'bring you to everlasting life' and 'salvation, unto life eternal' have deeply influenced worship and are most obviously interpreted in the sense of individuals going to heaven after death.[83] The present and future worlds are often strongly contrasted and the world to come is defined in terms of heavenly everlasting life. The future restoration of creation is not exactly denied, but it is omitted in the traditional liturgies in order to emphasise the personal entry to heaven by a believer at the point of death.

Preparing for worship

So as you work to prepare worship for Sunday, and if you wish to include more of the doctrine of creation, you may find material to help you in the ten elements I have offered. This outline slices through may key aspects of Christian doctrine, and therefore affects the way we think about them. It deals with God's relationship with his creation in his transcendence, providence and presence. It touches on the persons and activity of the Father, the Son and the Spirit. It covers the relationship between the human and non-human creation and the effect of sin on the natural world. It covers the redemption of the created order through Christ and its final destiny.

A number of significant theological tensions have been raised as we have considered these ten elements. They are reflected to some extent in the words spoken in public worship in older traditional liturgies, as we have illustrated. But these tensions have also begun to appear frequently in contemporary worship services, which, for a variety of reasons, are incorporating creation themes. Some are merely influenced by an interest in the natural environment, or concerns about ecological matters. The fact is that Christians from many traditions are beginning more deliberately to include such matters in worship. Some of these efforts are more successful than others. Some of them are positively strange, perhaps even destructive to the faith of the church. In the next chapter we examine some examples of these contemporary new approaches and we will try to discern what is of value in them and what lessons may be learned for public worship in our own contexts.

5

Contemporary Efforts – Problems and Possibilities

Public worship in the contemporary church is beginning to change in response to the challenges of the environmental crisis. As people generally become more aware of the need to live with sensitivity to the natural world, new material is entering Christian worship and influencing the thinking of those who plan and lead services. In this chapter we consider some examples of these changes of practice in order to glean ideas and to flag up possible dangers. We also discuss some other matters that are part of more traditional liturgies and that contain significant dangers as worship begins to adapt to the new environmental challenge. But before we proceed, we need to bear in mind a number of preliminary points.

First, nothing in this field of discussion is ever entirely bad or entirely good. Perfect worship only exists in heaven. If you go to a church service, it is possible that you are entirely delighted and helped by everything. It is more likely, however, that the service will strike you as a mixture of helpful things and not so helpful things. So in discussing various worship practices and liturgies, we will find much of value, but also much that is dubious, and it is these dubious things that need to be assessed carefully. In this chapter our focus is on the dangers of new practices, but that does not mean that there is nothing of value to be gleaned. We will return to discuss the profitable aspects in Chapter 9.

Second, some of the material we look at is experimental and thus is likely to be 'out of the box' for Christian thinking, perhaps even quite disturbing to the average church worshipper. It is by exploring experimental and innovative worship practices like these, however, that we can more easily discern trends. Such material also contains ideas that might be used or suitably adapted for other contexts of public worship.

The nature and being of God

Some new liturgies and worship practices are inclined to confuse the being of God with the being of creation. We have already noted that a distinction between God in his essential being and the universe he has created is a fundamental element of Christian doctrine. To confuse God and the world in this way is to fall into the error of pantheism, that is, the belief that everything is God and that God is everything.

One of the criticisms of traditional worship by ecology-conscious Christians is that it distances God from the world in transcendence. They argue that his holy separation from the world is stressed at the expense of his immanence and that it is possible then to neglect to honour God as nearby, as involved and present with the ordinary physical things around us. A number of new forms of worship attempt to overcome this problem, but in some cases the new practices move so far in this direction that they fall into pantheism.

Celtic worship

Most popular and easy to discuss in this respect is the fresh approach to Christian public worship by what has come to be called 'Celtic worship'. You will almost certainly have been exposed to the influence of this movement, either in your own church or at special events. There is much to learn from it. It uses ancient traditions and contemporary sources to enable a fresh and creative spiritual life through the style and content of public worship. This movement is particularly significant, however, because it addresses some of the weaknesses of contemporary worship that we are exploring. Those who write for and encourage the use of Celtic worship give us good material to enable us to examine the relationship of worship and creation, for both its theological and practical implications.[1]

We may define Celtic corporate worship as worship that draws its liturgical content and style from hymns, prayers and spiritual poems that stand in a continually developing stream of material, some of which is from the early Celtic church but all of which is selected and shaped in relation to present needs since the late 1970s.[2] A number of liturgies for the daily office have been written and are used not only in the communities in which they originated, but also by others,[3] and the impact of such material is demonstrated by the inclusion of Celtic services in the Church of Scotland *Book of Common Order*.[4] At the very least, you may have experienced the revived use of an Irish blessing in church, or sung the Old Irish hymn, 'Be thou my vision, O Lord of my heart', sometimes played with urgent beating on a hand drum to create an ancient mood. Other contemporary songs and hymns have also appeared in the 'Celtic style'. There is thus value for our purposes in examining the theology of worship of the new Celtic spirituality and liturgy as one response to the need to introduce more creation themes into public worship.

The strong theology of creation that underlies Celtic worship is reflected in a heightened awareness of the natural world in the liturgy. This includes a desire to find God immanent in his creation and an ability to see the good already present in the created world and humanity. Widespread inclusion of creation themes may be confirmed by a brief glance at any book of Celtic liturgy. Almost invariably, the opening lines of any liturgy refer to God as creator, or to aspects of creation. So Iona liturgies include in the opening lines,

Leader	The God of heaven has made his home on earth,
All	CHRIST DWELLS AMONG US AND IS ONE WITH US.
Leader	Highest in all creation, he lives among the least . . .

Leader	O God, who called all life into being,
All	THE EARTH, SEA AND SKY ARE YOURS.
Leader	Your presence is all around us,
All	EVERY ATOM IS FULL OF YOUR ENERGY . . .

Leader   O God of all creation,
All   WHO HAS COME TO US IN JESUS . . .
                  (Iona Abbey Worship Book)[5]

The creation emphasis continually emerges in this way and therefore a number of the main elements of the doctrine of creation, which we analysed in the last chapter, are substantially present in this material.

Celtic liturgy and prayer also link worship and creation through deliberate connections to daily work and a continuous rhythm of sacrament and service, prayer and work.[6] The Northumbrian office for midday is designed to be read or recited 'in the time it takes to boil a kettle', while working or moving about.[7] The presence of God in daily life in Celtic spirituality

> was always mediated through some finite this-worldly reality, so that it would be difficult to imagine a spirituality more down-to-earth than this one . . . getting up, lighting the fire, going to work, going to bed, as well as birth, marriage, settling in a new house, death, were occasions for recognizing the presence of God.
>
> (*J. MacQuarrie*, Paths in Spirituality)[8]

Extending this attitude to corporate worship, some writers in this movement appeal for us to recover older traditions in which communal worship is linked to the land and rural working life. They urge the reintroduction of Harvest, Lammas, Rogation days and Plough Sunday, all of which have agricultural connections, arguing for a 'thoroughly creation affirming spirituality' that is not fearful to bless the ground, and sees the church as mediating the spiritual dimension of life to their community.[9] These are good themes to consider and we shall return to them in Chapter 10.

Along with these very significant positive aspects of Celtic worship, which have arisen partly as a response to the challenge of ecological concern, we need to attend to the possible dangers of this theology and its liturgy. The pantheistic tendency finds a ready home here, particularly in places where imagery and metaphor overtake the thought. The theology of the early Celtic church sustained a firm Trinitarian theology but, 'The sense of God's immanence in his creation was so strong in Celtic spirituality as to amount sometimes almost to a pantheism.'[10]

Part of this problem today is the inclusion in some Celtic prayers and liturgies of material from other faiths and philosophies: the process of syncretism, stemming from the idea, present in many faiths, that in the end all religions and their gods are the same. This means that pantheistic concepts, present in this other material, have crept into Celtic prayers. An animist poem of the Celtic prince Ameregin is used in one collection; many old Gaelic poems have a similar mood; and there are links to Buddhist philosophy in which a 'sense of mindfulness' is created by belief in the presence of God in all things.[11] Some defend these prayers and hold that it is pan*en*theism and not pantheism that lies behind Christian Celtic writing – that is, not the belief that God is identified with all things, but that God is in some sense 'in' all things.[12] This is similar to the idea we discussed earlier about the presence of God by the Holy Spirit within his creation and might, in many lines of liturgy, be happily affirmed.

However, the influence of the pantheistic tendency upon Celtic liturgy is profound. There is a perceived attempt in some writers to 're-ignite native spiritualities' with links in the literature to Amerindian, Australian Aboriginal, and Druidic poetry and theology.[13] The Celtic liturgies lead in a few places to apparent identification of natural phenomenon with God, without correction. In one prayer we read,

> Great eye of the Great God . . .
> Glory to thee, Thou glorious sun.
> Glory to thee, Thou sun, Face of the God of life.
>
> (*Carmina Gadelica*)[14]

In another liturgy we have,

> Deep peace of the running wave to you,
> Deep peace of the flowing air to you,
> Deep peace of the quiet earth to you . . .

And then further,

> May the peace of the night enfold me so that I may be bathed in love.
>
> (*Robson*, A Celtic Liturgy)[15]

A further related problem is that in many prayers we lose the usual names for God for more indistinct ones, such as, 'O being of life, O being of peace, O being of time, O being of eternity'.[16] If surrounded with statements about the transcendence of God, or with biblical titles for God, these phrases do not carry great weight – and overall a vision of a transcendent yet intimate God does appear in the Celtic material. However, the potential for confusion of the being of God with the being of creation is clearly present in these prayers and titles, especially where it is not immediately corrected or balanced. The problem is multiplied if such metaphors and images are frequent. In Chapter 9 we shall return to the important question of creation metaphors and how they can best be used.

New ecological liturgies

Although the loss of Trinitarian titles is not a major problem in most books of Celtic prayer and liturgy, a problem does arise when similar language is used in many of the new ecological liturgies, as in material from the North American Conference on Religion and Ecology[17] and resources offered for an annual Earth Day and other similar occasions.[18] For these events, the text is almost totally devoted to ecological matters and therefore a doctrine of creation is implicit in almost every sentence.[19] As a result, it is possible to discern in some detail the theology of creation represented by them. The basic assumption of these services is that the church prays and acts in harmony with and on behalf of the whole of the created order. Again, much of this material is valuable and is entirely biblical and orthodox. For example, in one Earth Day prayer we have a clear address to a sovereign God,

> Loving God, loving God,
> all creation calls you blessed . . .

then lines that stress his immanence through pneumatology,

> Your Spirit imprints the whole universe with life and mystery . . .

and a final request that God will

> Open our hearts to understand
> the intimate relationship that you have with all creation.
> > (*Source unknown*, 'Psalm of the Cosmos')[20]

In this particular prayer a good balance is maintained between the reality of God as the sovereign transcendent creator and God as immanent, dwelling intimately with his creation by the Spirit. But worship of the immanent God needs to be treated with caution. Without corresponding honour of the transcendent Creator there is the potential for such prayers and texts to be pure pantheism.

In these liturgies God's immanence appears with regularity. The quotation in Acts 17:28 is turned into a prayer: 'In you we live and move and have our being';[21] God is 'the energy that moves all things'[22] and his 'hands are upon all creatures who live upon the earth'.[23] God is, 'the mystery that lives in us, that is the ground of every unique expression of life, the source of fascination that calls all things to communion'.[24]

These phrases can be defended as being not pantheistic, but panentheistic. However, words of Annie Dillard, offered as a prayer meditation in an Earth Day service in 1992, seem to move beyond that: 'It could be that god has not absconded but spread, as our vision and understanding of the universe have spread, to a fabric of spirit and sense so grand and subtle, so powerful in a new way, that we can only feel blindly its hem.'[25]

This 'god', now spelt without a capital letter, has spread into the fabric of the universe and is unknown. This meditation not only departs substantially from the doctrine of transcendence, but calls into question the existence of a personal creator God of any kind. The same is true of a 'Litany of Gratitude' from the Web of Creation website, which reads,

Leader	We live in all things.
	All things live in us.
Response	We rejoice in all life.

Leader	We live by the sun.
	We move with the stars.
Response	We rejoice in all life.

('A Litany of Gratitude')[26]

Many similar prayers begin with no form of address and no reference to God at all, or he is addressed merely in general, not specifically in Christian terms. Some prayers are not so much to God as creator, but to the earth itself. They are an act of communion with the physical earth rather than the God who made it. In one litany the first responses run:

Leader	To bring new life to the land
	To restore the waters
	To refresh the air
Response	We join with the earth and with each other.

('A Litany for Healing')[27]

The following five sections move in similar vein. This particular prayer is a meditation on the need for the healing of the earth and human instrumentality in that healing, but contains no direct reference to God. It is a valuable and much- needed thought in a world that cries out for human behaviour to change so that healing can come to the earth. In this prayer, however, the concept of God as creator, and as the one who makes healing possible, is effectively removed in favour of healing through human harmony with nature. It is very different from the psalmist's vision of Yahweh 'who heals all your diseases'[28] and of the prophets who saw healing of the land as ultimately God's action through which the nation was to be blessed.[29]

In these liturgies the immanence of God extends to a concept of the 'web of creation' or the 'web of life' in which nothing is independent or self-sufficient. Therefore, the need for a proper relationship of the human to the non-human creation also appears. The liturgies reflect this: 'a web that cannot be broken without injury to all', 'the fragile balance of life', 'this precious web of life', 'our lives intertwined with', and so on. The danger for Christian doctrine here is that such a view of world order may dissolve into monism, that is, the idea that all spiritual and physical things are one. This is, in fact, what happens if no specific reference to God appears, such as in one prayer where,

> We join with the earth and with each other.
> We join together as many diverse expressions of one loving mystery: for the healing of the earth and the renewal of all life.
>
> ('A Litany for Healing')[30]

Or, in a suggested Amerindian meditation,

> Whatever befalls the earth
> befalls the children of the earth.
> Man did not weave the web of life;
> He is merely a strand in it.
> Whatever he does to the web,
> He does to himself.
>
> (*Chief Seattle*)[31]

The absence of references to God and his creative power and self-sufficient transcendence becomes problematic in a Christian context. Some texts are better balanced, so that we have also,

> Leader   For the joy of being a part of nature
>   throughout all our days and in all our ways,
> Response   We praise you, O God.
>
> ('Litany for Growth')[32]

Here, although the term 'nature', rather than 'your creation', might be questioned as implying some separate or independent status for the natural world, the basic balance is good: that human beings are in harmony with the created world as God's creatures among creatures, and that God is to be praised for it all.

In a healthy desire to include thought about the presence of God in creation, contemporary liturgies often deliberately alter traditional or biblical phrases. This can lead to a loss of a vision of the transcendent God who is revealed uniquely in Christ. One translation of the Lord's Prayer included in a New Zealand Maori Anglican liturgy begins,

> Eternal Spirit,
> Earth-maker, Pain-bearer, Life-giver,
> Source of all that is and that shall be,
> Father and Mother of us all,
> Loving God, in whom is heaven:
> The hallowing of your name echoes through the universe!
>
> (New Zealand Prayer Book)[33]

Here the authors do not wish to place God at a distance, as in the usual 'Our Father in heaven, hallowed be your name'. Rather, they wish to stress his deep involvement in the processes of the earth and daily life. The motive may be good, but the immediate effect is loss of transcendence. As a single instance of prayer for a special occasion, this loss is not particularly significant. It may be regarded as a helpful corrective and a way of expressing that true and eternal life is to be found in God, as in Jesus' prayer, 'And this is eternal life, that they may know you, the only true God.'[34] If, however, this language is standard in a community, and if it is part of a liturgy that makes many such changes, the absence of a vision of the transcendent God becomes important.

In a further example, in an unofficial Anglican Eucharistic liturgy the Preparation for Communion reads:

> Spirit of Light and Love,
> Essence of all being,
> Fullness and truth,
> Hope of all ages,
> You are the Eternal One,
> Revealed in many forms,
> Worthy of our adoration,
> In this and all worlds,
> In time and eternity.
>
> (*J. Robinson*, Celebration)[35]

In this prayer the language of transcendence is avoided. Emphasis is placed on the Spirit present with the worshippers, rather than on the Creator or King of the universe. The phrases in this prayer deliberately exclude hierarchical and gender implications, leaving open a perception of an impersonal Spirit-God who is somehow 'revealed in many forms', to be found in the world around. Later parts of this service use traditional language, so the difficulty is not true of the whole Eucharist, but this prayer illustrates that when we try to be more conscious of creation and express God's immanence, the result may be a loss of transcendence and perhaps of a clear distinction between God and the created world. This clearly has implications for the doctrines of incarnation and redemption.

The Trinitarian titles

A further issue in public worship that reflects contemporary concerns, particularly where people are eager to be aware of creation, is the loss of the Trinitarian names for God. It is common practice now to replace the Trinitarian titles with other terms, such as 'Earth-maker, Pain-bearer, Life-giver' in the prayer quoted on page 83. In this version of the Lord's Prayer the Trinitarian relationship between the Father and the human Christ is lost. In the gospel understanding Jesus utters the prayer with us so that 'our Father' is his Father too, but Trinitarian theology is abandoned here in favour of a merely metaphorical reading of God as 'Father and Mother of us all'.

The practice of finding new names for the Trinitarian God carries the possibility of great misunderstanding. The intention of such rephrasing is to reflect something fresh about God's nature in relation to his created world. The idea is to help worshippers identify the God of the prayer with the experiences of their own lives: as creatures, as bearers of pain and as aware of the presence of God in all things. This is a worthwhile task. Such titles, however, especially if used continually, place everything in the worshippers' present experiences of God. They put revelation through Christ the Son at a remove, and may even imply a denial of the distinctions of the three persons of the Trinity. The Trinitarian creedal titles of Father, Son and Spirit, by contrast, deeply connect to the gospel story and display the three persons in their distinct relations within the Godhead.

It is unnecessary for leaders and pastors to be over cautious about titles for God. We need not exclude such new language entirely. There is value, for a single instance, in replacing the address to Father, Son and Spirit, and those used in the example on page 83 are both inventive and helpful. Habitual use of other titles in place of the Trinitarian ones has, however, become common in the kind of liturgy we are discussing here. One serious motive is to avoid the masculine terminology that the traditional titles contain. But such practice diminishes Trinitarian theology and removes the vision of the gospel narrative that stands behind these titles. It is the person of the Son and his unique relation to the Father as both human and divine that provides the most secure theological foundation for relating Christian public worship and creation. To abandon the carefully framed Trinitarian language of the church is to risk losing what it was created to safeguard.

There are many cases of implied or overt pantheism in these liturgies, particularly in the Earth Day worship material. However, in general they do maintain a balance between transcendence and immanence. The Celtic liturgies generally are balanced in this respect, with an emphasis on both creation and the immanence of God within a Trinitarian structure and with a clear sense of God's transcendence. Therefore these liturgies, on the whole, may be regarded as a needed corrective in the corporate worship of the church, both for special ecological occasions and for general use.

Christ and creation

A further issue emerges in a number of the newer worship practices and liturgies that seek to take account of the ecological crisis. It is the identification of Christ with the creation in a way that diminishes his divinity. One example from the Celtic movement

illustrates this tendency. Christ is seen in one liturgy as the fulfilment of the 'green man' tradition of English ecology.[36] This idea
appears at the beginning of a Eucharist, in a mysterious phrase,
which reads,

> Risen Christ, we welcome you. You are the flowering bough of cre-
> ation; from you cascades music like a million stars, truth to cleanse
> a million souls.
>
> ('A Celtic Eucharist')[37]

Christ spoken of as 'the flowering bough of creation', quite apart
from being unusual and over-sentimental, contains the implication that he is the result of the budding and flowering of some
part of God's creation. The phrase itself does not make clear the
distinction between creation and the uncreated incarnate Son,
nor do the lines and prayers surrounding it explain the concept.
The understanding of Christ as incarnate God and the precise
mode of his human nature need attention here.

This is only a mildly worrying example in comparison with
other worship practices that identify Christ with God's creation.
More serious is a suggested meditation in the Earth Day liturgies
that includes material from the 'Stations of the Cross' by
Matthew Fox in which

> participants took a map of the Earth and nailed its four corners to
> a cross and erected the cross on the top of the sand dune as the
> wind howled through us. With the nailing to the cross, the pound-
> ing echoing along the beach, the . . . memory of Jesus crucified
> awakened.
>
> (*Matthew Fox*, Creation Spirituality)[38]

Here the body of Christ is identified with the earth and the cruci-
fying carries the notion that the earth suffers and is crucified as
Christ. The difficulty is that Christ is not the earth. He cannot be
equated with the earth. Having taken up created flesh into his
divine nature, he bears the suffering of created and fallen beings
and thus the suffering of the earth, but he is not to be identified
in his whole being with that which he has himself created sover-
eignly. It has its own nature.

Tree-planting Eucharist

How do you respond to the concept of a 'tree-planting Eucharist'? This is so far outside the thinking and experience of most Christians that we are likely to reject it as a joke. But such services are now being used in a number of places, particularly in the USA and Canada. Forms of worship were developed and promoted in Zimbabwe in the 1990s to work out this concept.[39] The Zimbabwean Institute of Religious Research and Ecological Conservation (ZIRRCON) engaged with churches and traditional religions to plant 1.2 million trees in hundreds of woodlots. Marthinus Daneel, a South African missionary and theologian working in Zimbabwe, encouraged the churches in 'the war of the trees' as an ecological application of the kingdom of God.[40] Daneel and others then developed worship material to inspire and educate the churches and associated organisations in ecological responsibility. These forms of worship are therefore of interest in providing a basis for theological discussion on the relationship between creation and worship.

Much can be learned from considering the worship ideas and material from Daneel and ZIRRCON and we shall return to draw out some of these valuable lessons later. Our concern at present is to illustrate how this approach to worship can produce a confused Christology, in particular in the justification for the tree-planting Eucharist. Christ is the redeemer of both humanity and the earth since through Christ and his cross God chose to reconcile all things to himself.[41] In these Eucharist services in Zimbabwe, immediately after receiving the bread and wine, the congregation goes out to plant a sapling in a nearby woodlot. This is held to demonstrate the connection of Christ's redeeming work to both humanity and the earth. In one liturgy we find,

> We are reconciled with creation
> Through the body and blood of Jesus
> Which brings peace,
> He who came to save
> All creation.
>
> (*Marinder in* African Earthkeepers)[42]

The argument is as follows: harmony between human beings and creation has been destroyed by human sin; Christ came to bring peace through the cross so that a new harmonious relationship can be established between humanity and the earth as well as with God; this new relationship is expressed after the Eucharist by planting a sapling in the 'Lord's acre'.

The forgiveness and reconciliation of humanity to God is central, but this reconciliation is worked out by human activity in ecological harmony and care. The cross is therefore the means by which reconciliation between humanity and God's creation is made. Sins against the earth and its creatures are forgiven and the reconciling act of planting and restoring the earth has meaning. The sermon during the liturgy states: 'Today we plant trees as an act of reconciliation between us and all creation, in Jesus Christ. We thank him for his atonement, which makes this act of reconciliation possible.'[43]

Connecting Eucharist and tree-planting in one ceremony is therefore very significant theologically. A further liturgy states, 'Our Eucharist of tree-planting symbolises Christ's salvation of all creation, for in him all things hold together.'[44] The Eucharist is a combined task involving remembrance of Christ and tree-planting. The blood shed to forgive ecological sins is followed by discipleship expressed in a simple act of ecological care. In Zimbabwe at that time, and no doubt in many other places, the need for the preservation of trees and renewal of the woodlands and forests was fundamental to the whole future life of the community.

Ecological discipleship

Thus far the connection between the work of Christ on the cross and ecological action is expressed in words that are no different from any that may be said after any Communion service. Daneel's tree-planting Eucharist is accompanied by a call to discipleship: 'Go out and love as Christ loved you, serve as he has served you, work for reconciliation and justice, as you have been reconciled to God in Christ.' We strike a problem, however, when we look at how this practice is seen in relation to the person of Christ. The justification given as the 'cornerstone' of this Eucharist is that Christ is the connection between the earth and the church because these are two manifestations of his body. In the Eucharist worshippers receive the elements and in so doing 'accept responsibility for the repair of the cosmic body of Christ, to which they belong and which they too have abused'.[45]

In the African context of Zimbabwe there is a particular reason for such a theology. In the local religious traditions of the Shona, among whom Daneel was working, as in many traditions, the tribal ancestors are identified with certain aspects of the physical environment. They are seen not merely as guardians of the soil, rivers, trees and animals, but as having strong personal associations with these aspects of the natural environment and with protective powers over them. Daneel's purpose in extending this idea is to try to make a link between African ancestor veneration and the Christian understanding of the person of Christ. Christ thus becomes the 'great ancestor', the ultimate Lord of a hierarchy of former spirits of the tribal dead. In the same way as they are connected with individual parts of the local environment in their limited spheres, so Christ, as the 'great ancestor', is identified with the whole, with the soil and the totality of the physical world around.

The body of Christ

Jürgen Moltmann, in his ecological theology, shows how humanity is being formed in the image of Christ, a condition that is to be attained fully only in the last days in God's eternal kingdom. In this future, Christian believers, fully redeemed and acting as agents of God in the image of Christ, will have a role that includes 'ruling with Christ' over animals and the earth. This final ruling of humanity over the natural world means that there is a motive in applying Christ's redemptive work in present ecological responsibility.[46] Daneel, however, extends this idea to include the concept of the earth as one dimension of the body of Christ.[47] This theological background emerges in liturgies, in one case including the clearly heretical idea,

> God the Father created the earth and Christ was part of it.
> (African Earthkeepers)[48]

There are severe difficulties with this Christology. First, it seems to confuse the being of Christ as God with the being of creation and therefore, as in the line above, implies that Christ came into being as part of God's first creation. There is a much better way of expressing how God in Christ is related to his material creation and reflecting it in worship, but it is not in identifying the human nature of Christ with the earth by viewing it as the body of Christ. The solution lies in a more carefully expressed doctrine of Christ.

A second difficulty raised by the idea of the 'cosmic body of Christ' is that it diminishes the importance of the Holy Spirit in relation to creation. The presence of God in creation is to be viewed as the presence of the Spirit of God working in and upon all that he has made. Daneel has attempted to take the central aspects of the Christian faith, which are expressed in the Eucharist, and link them directly to ecological responsibility. He has done this by identifying the 'Eucharistic body', the church around the communion table, with the 'ecological body', the earth with its need for human stewardship and care. The church is indeed the 'body of Christ' in a unique unity with him. But the one who unites his body, the church, at the Eucharist is not to be confused with the physical earth. The solution lies in a more robust doctrine of the Spirit in relation to the creation. The same Spirit who animates and unites the church as the body of Christ also gives life and purpose to the created world, which is Christ's creation. The closeness to God, in both Eucharist and ecological action, which Daneel seeks is not so much the presence of Christ, as the presence of the Holy Spirit in both church and creation. It is not found by identifying the earth as a form of the body of Christ.

Blessing

One way of thinking about how God is at work in his creation is through the concept of blessing. But this also contains a problem because of the way that it has been worked out in public worship. In the Genesis narrative, when God creates the living creatures on the fifth day, he blesses them and commands them to multiply and fill the earth. Similarly, after all the work of creation is finished, the first human beings are placed on earth and immediately God's blessing is placed upon them, so that they will be fruitful and multiply and rule over creation on his behalf.[49]

All things are blessed

In the Eastern Orthodox worship tradition the concept of blessing features strongly. The people worship in the physical church building, which is presented as an image of the whole universe.[50] The whole universe, angels, saints, animals and all natural things, are present, joining with the church at worship. The act of public worship in the liturgy represents and includes all acts, all of life and all natural things. Worship, therefore, is 'an all-inclusive attitude, embracing every object and every moment'.[51] The whole of life is viewed as holy, so that,

> In the immense cathedral which is the universe of God, every person, whether scholar or manual labourer, is called to act as the priest of his or her whole life – to take all that is human and turn it into an offering and a hymn of glory.[52]

The act of blessing the people in the liturgical process is at the heart of this broad and all-pervasive and holy presence of God in life in its variety. Blessing demonstrates the openness that exists between heaven and earth and connects worship to the world beyond the church and to God as creator in the events of daily life. So we have a blessing at the end of the liturgy,

> O Lord, you bless those who bless you . . . Give peace to your world, to your priests, to our rulers, and to all your people. For every good gift and every perfect gift is from on high, coming down from you, the Father of lights; and to you we give glory.
> (The Divine Liturgy)[53]

This blessing recognises the gifts of God in natural life and represents in words of blessing the open connection from the liturgy to the extended place of God's activity in the world.

Pathway to ordinary life

Two other events that take place in the Orthodox liturgy also show God's blessing on the daily life of the people and emphasise the relationship between spiritual and physical things. These are the giving of the *prosphoron*, which means 'offering', and the *antidoron*, the gift after the service. Quite early in the history of the church it became the practice for the people to bring forward the bread and wine for the communion at the start of a service. This gradually evolved into the Orthodox ceremony of the Great Entrance, the event at the heart of the Orthodox liturgy that enacts the entry of Christ the Logos into the world in his incarnation.[54] The *prosphoron*, the gift of bread, is brought from the hearth and home to the church for use in the Communion and received by the priest in an opening 'liturgy of preparation'. Worship and ordinary life are deeply connected at this point as a pathway is made into the worship from creation, home and human craft. The same pathway is formed at the opposite end of the liturgy through the practice of the *antidoron*. In this part of the service, which is taken up enthusiastically by the congregation, blessed bread not used for the Eucharist is distributed to the congregation at the end of the liturgy.[55]

The practice of the *prosphoron* and the *antidoron* reflects an openness of the natural to the eternal, the blessing of God upon all of life that is characteristic of Orthodoxy. Standing at the beginning and close of the liturgy, they frame the whole with a sense of God's blessing on the created world and on the industry and society of human life.

The elevation and blessing of physical objects play a major role in Orthodoxy, and are good habits, reflecting the blessing of God upon his first creation and his continual blessing ever since. In practice, however, such an emphasis contains a serious problem.[56] The unhealthy separation between supposedly religious and non-religious life, which often seems to underlie many kinds of religious thinking, including Christian theology, is not fully overcome by the common practice of blessing people and physical things.

The Orthodox practice of blessing is not confined to public worship in the liturgy. It is part of the regular duty of the priests, as in many traditions. One example we can helpfully discuss is the Great Blessing of Waters on 6 January, an ancient ceremony that commemorates and acts out Jesus' baptism by John the Baptist in the River Jordan. In Orthodoxy Jesus' baptism is seen as having cosmic significance, not just significance for Jesus himself. It is a revelation of the Trinity: the Father speaking, the Son being baptised and the Spirit descending on him. It reflects Jesus' incarnation, an act of redeeming obedience in which he enters the fallen creation to cleanse and sanctify it. Water is the 'cosmic element' and in the Orthodox ceremony of the Great Blessing it is made holy by the descent of the Holy Spirit upon it.[57]

This ceremony, with the liturgy that accompanies it, raises a key question about all 'blessing' of material things. One approach is to say that to 'bless' an object means to change something about the object itself, and therefore to change the effect it has when someone uses it or touches it. Does God act in some way upon the material matter being blessed to give it something that it did not have before? That is certainly the idea that lies behind the Orthodox ceremony of the Great Blessing. The text of the liturgy declares a change in the water itself. The priest asks,

> For this water to be sanctified by the power and operation and
>   visitation of the Holy Spirit, let us pray to the Lord.
> For there to come down upon these waters the cleansing operation
>   of the
>   Trinity beyond all being, let us pray to the Lord.
> For there to be given them the grace of redemption, the blessing of
>   Jordan, let us pray to the Lord.
>   (*From the* Great Blessing of the Waters)[58]

In this whole liturgy a number of changes are expected through the blessing of the water. It will be 'sanctified', have 'cleansing' and be given 'grace', and those who drink the water, or are sprinkled with it, are then similarly sanctified or given grace. Basil of Caesarea, a fourth-century bishop, is regarded as the author of these prayers. He states that through the priest's blessing the water receives a 'quickening power of the Holy Spirit'.[59] Ambrose of Milan agrees, using the troubling of the Pool of Bethesda as his support.[60] There is thus a long history in support of this approach: that blessing an object, especially water, alters the very nature of the thing blessed and conveys that blessing to those touched by it.

Glory in everything

There is, however, a better way of viewing the act of blessing physical things. Blessing an object or a person reaffirms as good and blessed and under God's approval those things that he created and blessed at the beginning of creation. The natural world in which we live, and human life itself, although spoiled by sin, can still be the objects of our wonder at the beauty and goodness placed there by God. The act of blessing changes the people who use the objects and their attitudes to them, not the objects themselves. Blessing is thus 'a proclamation that the universe around us is not a chaos, but a cosmos. There is glory in everything; this is a world full of wonder'.[61]

The act of blessing is thus a proclamation in prayer that sets the person blessing or being blessed in a new orientation to God and his creation. In addition, the act of blessing looks to the final end of creation. The ultimate truth about the natural world is that it is being led on to perfection, that it is destined for reconciliation with God through Christ. Looked at in this way, the Great Blessing of Waters has become a celebration of creation for the Orthodox Church, an act that asserts the goodness and value of the environment and helps to change our attitudes and behaviour towards it.[62] In representing the theology of blessing in this way, worship and creation are brought into a productive relationship. Our world and all that is in it, threatened as it is by human misbehaving, needs to be blessed in this way with our words and our actions.

The practice of blessing things, when not understood in this way, can be very different. The main emphasis in many traditions, commonly understood from the widespread practice of blessing objects, is that of making creation holy for human use. When it is popularly used as a way of making material items 'more holy', the idea of blessing severs the sense of God's blessing upon his whole creation and reserves it for the blessed items.[63] Even some Orthodox theologians struggle at this point with the Orthodox interpretation of the practice of blessing.[64] Nicholas Lossky points out that in the Genesis account of the creation of the first human being, the life-giving presence of the Spirit was breathed into him by the Creator, who 'breathed into his nostrils the breath of life'.[65] The Spirit is therefore present in the creation of human beings, as well as of all creation, and is now continually at work in them to enable a free and loving response. Lossky therefore views the sanctifying that occurs in all blessing not as applying to the physical object that is being blessed, but as upon the worshipper by the Holy Spirit. It is a change of perspective within the human soul. This leads to care for creation expressed by: 'charitable hearts . . . aflame with love for all creation . . . for the birds, for the beasts, for all creatures'.[66] The practice of blessing is thus a reaffirmation of the first blessing on living creatures and humanity asserted in Genesis.[67] It broadens a view of creation as holy in all its dimensions when rightly perceived by the believer.

Another Orthodox theologian, Alexander Schmemann, points out that blessing, when looked at as a sanctifying act, blurs the distinction between the sacramental and the non-sacramental in worship. On the one hand, it deprives the sacrament of its unique place in the Christian's life and, on the other, creates something mysterious or 'special' about the act of blessing natural things.[68]

There is therefore a tension between acts of blessing as they are used in practice and justified in Orthodoxy and the broader theology of the Orthodox Churches. In this, all creation is robustly affirmed and considered the object of God's blessing. The Spirit is at work sustaining, perfecting and uniting all creation to humanity and finally to God. Nor is God's blessing restricted to believers. God blessed the whole of the human race with his bounty and with physical life in all its variety. Blessing is thus given to a person as 'a creature among creatures' and, in turn, to all living things. So any special act of God's revelation and salvation 'acquires its horizon in God's all embracing activity'.[69] It is not just in saving intervention and deliverance that God works, but in continuing and general activity in his creation.

Blessing and the cross

The Roman Catholic Church has solved this tension by linking God's blessing solely to the central sacrament of the Mass. Because the Eucharist is the heart of Roman liturgy, the blessing of God is primarily to be received in the reception of the bread during the Mass. All blessings uttered by the priest in the Eucharist, and at any other sacramental moment, are regarded as aspects of the blessing of God that is enhanced by Christ who entered into creation to make all things holy.[70] There are therefore 'sacramentals' in the Roman Church, lesser signs that surround the sacraments, and that are 'occasions' for the grace received through the sacraments to take hold of us and for Christ's life to deepen in us.[71]

So, for example, blessed ashes (linked to the Sacrament of Penance) and the blessing of rings (linked to the Sacrament of Marriage) are ways in which 'various occasions in life are rendered holy'.[72] Each sacramental is linked with one of the seven sacraments of the church and each sacrament is dependent on the highest sacrament, the Sacrament of the Mass. All are thus part of the saving, sanctifying and redeeming work of God through Christ.

Blessing seen in this way is fundamental to all worship in the Roman scheme, but the outcome is again to separate the thing blessed from the rest of material creation. Blessing life and sanctifying it through the sacramentals at first appears to affirm the value of natural processes, such as the married relationship, childbirth and physical objects, for Christian use. The opposite, however, is true. Blessing is theologically linked not to the work of God in creation, or to the work of Christ as the agent of creation, but to the redeeming sacrifice of the cross, since it depends on the Eucharistic sacrifice of the Mass at the centre.[73] Sacramental blessings may be understood as showing that all things are under the rule of Christ and are used in dependence on him, as the Orthodox views discussed above demonstrate. But in the Roman scheme of blessing, these particular things are made holy or acceptable for use only in a redemptive connection. This pushes to one side God's wider blessing of all creation;[74] it is not in harmony with the words of Jesus who declared all foods clean;[75] nor is it consonant with apostolic teaching, which affirms that all food, and thus all the gifts of God, are to be received with thankful hearts.[76]

The practice of blessing in public worship is certainly a key to enhancing the relationship of worship and creation and engendering in human life a sense of the holiness and value of all created things. It is certainly to be encouraged and developed – but as an affirmation of the goodness of creation and not as a way of selecting out some things for special sanctification. This is an important theme and one to which we will return (see page 148).

In this chapter we have tried to point out some of the ways in which Christian corporate worship is responding to the arrival of the contemporary environmental challenge. We have noted some helpful and creative forms of worship and new liturgies that are beginning to influence the church at worship. We have also noted that serious dangers emerge when we try to incorporate creation themes and an awareness of the natural world into public worship – fundamental aspects of Christian doctrine may be adapted or changed as a result of such liturgy and worship. On the one hand, this is true in particular of newer and more experimental liturgies and in the theological justifications offered for them. On the other hand, some aspects of the long and eminent tradition of liturgy of the older churches may need further consideration, such as in the Roman Catholic Church and the Orthodox Churches. These have evolved their own ways of holding creation within the context of public worship, but in the light of current thinking about the environment and the doctrine of creation some further thought on these matters is needed.

A better theological justification for the relationship of humanity to the environment is possible and better ways of expressing this relationship in our public worship and liturgy can be found. We have discussed some unhelpful and theologically dangerous ways of seeking to do so, but there are also theologically healthy and more productive approaches. It is to these that we now turn.

6

Worship in the Humanity of Christ

We have discussed some of the difficulties that emerge as Christians in various traditions and in contemporary experiments in public worship have tried to place worship in relation to God and his creation. The best way for Christians to think about this issue is to see how the worship of the Creator by the creature is illuminated by the divine–human person of Jesus Christ. This exploration returns to questions with which we began in Chapter 1. How is the worship of the church related to the ordinary life of the Christian beyond the church? What is the person who is not a believer in Christ (or not yet a believer) doing in Christian public worship? And most important: How is what we do in Sunday services properly related to the environmental challenge the world faces?

We can take the second of these questions as an example. On a passing visit your aunt Jane, her husband and a couple of adult cousins express interest in coming with you to your church on Sunday. They are not practising Christians. They are happy living without any kind of religious faith, as far as you know. They sit with you in the row and respectfully join in as best they can with the songs, prayers and other aspects of the service. At some times in the service they seem just to be listening, but at other times they seem to be more engaged, more personally involved. They say the Lord's Prayer with an apparent sense of meaning. They join in heartily with at least a couple of the songs. You notice that these do not contain any direct reference to Christ, but are about the kingship, goodness and creative power of God. It seems that such matters are making more than a merely superficial connection with them.

The reflection that arises from a scene like this is whether Aunt Jane's response is anything that can be called genuine worship of the true and living God. In this chapter I want to argue that it is, that any person coming with sincerity and deliberate intention into such a setting does worship the living God at a preliminary level.

The same issue arises when we think about the way that public worship affects our daily lives. Is what is going on in church connected in any profitable or direct way with the issues of family, work, politics and leisure? How can these aspects of human life and earthly existence, particularly the worship of unbelievers as we have described it, be incorporated into public worship with practical wisdom and theological coherence? We need to do this without denying the very heart of Christian worship: its mediation through the eternal priesthood of Jesus Christ. This is the subject that will occupy us in this chapter.

In the Spirit and through the Son

All the main traditions of worship have understood that worship of the creator God is only possible through the mediation of Christ the Son. The theology of public worship has been worked out practically in a variety of ways in the different traditions, but the basic understanding is the same. In his talk with the woman at the well of Samaria, Jesus said that those who worship the Father must worship him in 'spirit and truth'. The meaning seems clear: such worship is possible only to those who acknowledge Jesus as the Christ because the Spirit by whom worship is made possible is given by Christ, and the truth needed for genuine worship is the truth of Christ. All worship of the Father is thus 'in the Spirit' and 'through the Son'.

Orthodox worship

The Eastern Orthodox tradition draws, it is argued, upon the very earliest Christian public worship. It consists of the weekly Sunday liturgy in which there is a special focus on the incarnation and the redeeming work of Christ the Logos. During the liturgy the worshippers contemplate 'the Holy Mystery' of

Christ's perfect person and work and as they respond in worship they make progress in the life of discipleship and holiness.[1]

The fundamental theological scheme of Orthodox worship is the story of God, and especially of the gospel of Christ, laid out and demonstrated in honour of the triune God. This story is the object of sustained contemplation and praise during the whole service, but at two special moments in the liturgy the story becomes the story of the worshipper. The first of these is the *epiclesis* (the 'calling upon') when the congregation invites the Spirit to fall upon the bread and wine and upon the whole congregation. The second is the Great Entrance, when the blessed bread is brought out into the body of the church as an enactment of the incarnation and a sign that Christ the Logos has become flesh like us and worked salvation for humanity and for creation through his perfect, obedient life, his atoning death and his resurrection. It is the incarnation of Christ and his redeeming work that makes it possible for created human beings, and with them all created things, to worship God.[2] This is worship offered to the Father through the Son.

Roman Catholic worship

The Roman Catholic theological scheme of public worship is very similar, but in this case renewed union with Christ that takes place in the course of the Mass is focused more directly upon the moment of reception of the bread and wine. It is all deeply linked to the story of redemption, but is more specifically connected to the suffering and atoning death of Christ. The story of God is laid out in the various parts of the liturgy, and in the preached word, and the worshippers enter into this story in thanksgiving and faith and by reception of the bread and wine.

The theology of worship that emerges in the Roman liturgy is based on the incarnation of Christ and the blessing available in the Eucharist, uniquely offered by the church. All God's natural gifts, represented in the gift of bread and wine used for the Eucharist, are viewed as good gifts created by Christ. They are then made holy in the enactment of the Mass, endowed with life and blessing and given back to the believer, conveying the grace and life of Christ in the moment of communion.[3]

In making the incarnation foundational to the worship in this way all human life and experience is marked as the object of redemption and God in Christ is shown to be deeply involved with the material of the created world. At the moment of communion, when the worshipper receives the sacrament, the divine life of God, offered now through Christ in the Eucharistic bread and wine, is given to the worshippers. They are united with God's eternal life as they receive again the body and blood of Christ.

So we see that in the Roman Catholic tradition, public worship is based on the same fundamental progression as in Orthodoxy. The worshipper is joined to Christ in his self-offering. Jesus' life, death and resurrection are presented to God in the worship. The church and all the worshippers present at the service and, to think more broadly, the whole of humanity and creation, are offered in worship to the Father in union with Christ's sacrifice.

Reformed worship

The theological scheme for the worship of the churches of the Reformation is similar in its purpose. The reformers rejected the Mass as a sacrifice, but deliberately set out in public worship to rehearse the gospel of Christ. It was to be presented through the two parts of the service, the word and the sacrament, so that Christ became the object of faith for the worshippers and a place of spiritual worship was found.

This strong and simple format for the construction of worship services largely continues today in churches of the western Protestant tradition. Public worship is seen as a meeting with a gracious God. Luther argued that worship is the experience of the blessing of God freely given through the gift of righteousness.[4] God is made known in Christ through the word read and preached and through the actions, prayers and reception of the bread and wine at Communion. Scripture reading and exposition are therefore significant in public worship in the Reformed churches. There is a strong emphasis both on the educative function of the services and on the moral strengthening that comes through teaching God's word and receiving the sacrament.

All of these benefits, however, depend on the offer of saving righteousness gained only through the merits of Christ. The individual's response of faith to that gospel promise is needed and this is renewed in every service as the word is preached and the sacrament is given. On that basis alone, through Christ alone, the worship of the congregation can be said to be true adoration of the living God.

The practical outworking of Reformed theology is different in the various liturgies and forms of worship that emerged from the Reformation, but the fundamental concept is the basis of worship on the gospel of Christ and his mediation. Public worship is a 'recapitulation' of the history of salvation in Christ[5] and a 'response to a Response already made for us and continually being made for us in Christ'.[6] Through the service people enter afresh into the experience of the gift of righteousness found in union with Christ, and so their worship is truly 'in the Spirit'.

Worship through Christ

A theology of corporate worship based on the gospel and the mediation of Christ is worked out practically in a different way in each of these three main traditions. Our task here is not to criticise them. I have outlined these three main theological traditions of worship in order to show that there is fundamentally a single scheme: corporate worship publicly sets out the given story of God, notably the story of God's saving and creating work through Christ, so that through him believers may enter afresh into the presence of God and worship him. The worshippers recount the glorious story in their thanksgiving and are joined again to Christ as they worship and as they respond by eating and drinking. The people at worship meet God afresh through the person of Christ and their praise, penitence, adoration and self-offering are joined into the self-offering of Jesus.

The basic theology of corporate worship that has existed in the church since the beginning is an interlacing of liturgical story and liturgical meeting. Corporate worship is thus a rehearsal, in praise before God, of the acts of his creating and saving work and a corporate meeting with God in various responses to that declaration or presentation. These responses include all the elements present in a service: praise, thanks, penitence, offering, submission to the word, rededication, commitment, yielding to the Spirit and so on.

Christian tradition

The important point for our purposes in all this is that the church in all its main traditions has taken the position that there is no true worship without the person of Christ, without the one true mediator. So how does worship connect with daily life and concern over the environment? Where does this leave Aunt Jane and the cousins who visited your church on that Sunday? Are they able to join in worship, or are they in fact just observers and interested listeners? The answer to these questions depends how you view what is usually called God's 'general revelation' of himself. General revelation, as distinct from 'special revelation', is what God reveals about himself, his nature, power and glory, in the things that exist. It is present all the time and needs no special intervention of God, no dramatic appearance of God or his representatives.

The psalmists speak of creation addressing humanity about God's nature. So in Psalm 19 we find that:

> The heavens are telling the glory of God;
> and the firmament proclaims his handiwork.

The apostle Paul seems to use arguments from general revelation in his gospel preaching to his pagan hearers. To the people of Lystra he speaks of 'the living God, who made the heaven and the earth and the sea and all that is in them', who 'has not left himself without a witness in doing good – giving you rains from heaven and fruitful seasons, and filling you with food and your hearts with joy'.[7] He speaks similarly in Athens of the creator God who has revealed something of himself so that people will 'search for God and perhaps grope for him and find him' and then quotes their own poet about God being not far from any one of us because 'In him we live and move and have our being.'[8] Again, Paul says of those who do not obey God that 'what can be known about God is plain to them, because God has shown it to them . . . through the things he has made' and through which 'his eternal power and divine nature, invisible though they are, have been understood'.[9] These scriptures are not extensive evidence for the doctrine of general revelation but, with a few notable exceptions, Christian thinkers have on the whole been persuaded that there is a general revelation of God to humanity.[10]

We need to proceed on the assumption, therefore, that God is able to convey something of himself to people through his creation, and through the simple fact of the existence of humanity on earth. There is special revelation, in particular the self-revealing of God through the incarnation of his Son Jesus Christ, but before and behind that there is general revelation. If this is so, then turning again to the subject of public worship, we can ask: Does the worship of God depend entirely on special revelation?

Two answers can be given to this question. The first is that worship of any kind is dependent on revelation of a special kind through God's intervention in the world in word or act. In this view, since Aunt Jane and the cousins, as far as can be discovered, are not aware of any such revelation or have not responded to it, then they are not able to worship God in any meaningful way. The second answer is that worship of God is part of what it means simply to be a created human being. We are all in the condition of 'createdness' in a created world. Arising from this recognition, general revelation produces a basic belief in God, which leads to worship of a general kind towards him as creator. As we have noted, the condemnation of God upon sinful humanity explained in Romans 1 is that they 'did not honour him as God or give thanks to him' (verse 21). Paul is arguing that humanity has seen God in his creative works and not responded in worship. This presupposes the ability to worship in a general way in response to general revelation.

In definitions of worship specifically Christological statements are often omitted so that worship is 'the response of the creature to the eternal',[11] or 'participation in the life of God in the mode appropriate to created being'.[12] So your visiting family standing in church are in fact making a meaningful response to the true and living God, but they do so on the ground of their created humanity.

The worship of the angels

A further dimension of worship on the basis of createdness opens up when we think about the worship that is offered to God by his angelic creation. Angels have been part of the scene of the worshipping church from early in its history. This argument does not depend on the actual existence of angels, which can be argued for elsewhere. Rather, we are discussing the theology that underlies Christian public worship. The place that the Christian Scriptures and tradition assign to angels in the worship of God indicates something important about the nature of worship and supports the argument here, whether or not you believe in the existence of angels. Angels, as described in Scripture, are created beings.[13] They are on the creation side of the fundamental divide between God and that which he creates. For example, the argument in Hebrews 1 is that angels, glorious as they are, are not divine as the Christ the Son is divine.[14] Also, angels are never described in the Bible as redeemed or needing redemption, and the plan and outcome of salvation are a mystery to them.[15] Yet they are consistently described as engaged in the worship of God. Their worship is therefore the worship of the created and not the redeemed.

The church in her public services early on understood that she joined in worship with the angelic hosts in heaven. Writing at the end of the first century, Clement of Rome exhorted Christians to good works since the angels with whom we worship 'stand ever ready to minister to His will'.[16] Cyril of Jerusalem (313–86) uses the worship of angels as part of his theology of the liturgy, and to justify the use of the *Sursum Corda* ('Lift up your hearts') and the *Trisagion* ('Holy, holy, holy'). We worship together, he says, so that we 'may be partakers with the hosts of the world above in their hymn of praise'.[17] In the Orthodox liturgies this idea appears strongly, so that earthly and heavenly worship are united and the whole universe – nature, humanity and angels – is drawn up through adoration into its final perfection.[18]

So if created angels are engaged in the worship of God, then the status of creatureliness is basic to all true worship. When a sinful human being, or fallen creation, offers worship to God through his redeeming acts this is a restoration and expansion of the worship of the creature. It is worship in a deeper dimension, now more complete because it is given new motive through the grace and saving acts of God in Christ, and leading to deeper human gratitude, praise and submission. As we have seen, if worship is entirely dependent on redemption in Christ, then angels would be excluded from such activity. Carson says that since angels worship, 'Worship cannot properly be defined as necessarily arising out of the gospel . . .The angels who orchestrate the worship of heaven do not offer their worship as a response to their experience of redemption.'[19]

But there is a contradiction here. If, as all the main traditions of the church have stressed, all true worship is mediated through the redemption and priestly work of Christ the Son of God, how can any worship that seems to be outside his work be true worship? Aunt Jane and the cousins in Sunday worship are again left simply as observers, or hearers, of the gospel. We need to review the place of Jesus Christ in this Sunday morning scene.

The nature of Christ

This contradiction leads us to a third aspect of this discussion. It is an argument arising from the human nature of Christ. We have already shown that in all the main traditions the worship of the Christian church is seen in relation to the gospel and therefore public worship is dependent on the self-offering and mediation of Christ. If the worship of the church is only by the mediation of the Son of God, then it does not at first seem to be available to those who do not believe in him. The only perfect worship in the universe is the worship, honour and submission of the Son to the Father and it is by incorporation into his perfect response to the Father that the church is able to offer her worship.

The idea that the Son 'worships' the Father may not sit easily with Christians wedded to the practice of worshipping Jesus Christ as the glorified Son of God, together with the Father and the Holy Spirit. The earthly life of Jesus, however, was a complete expression of the Christian's life of worship to God and a model of all that is done in Christian public worship. So, for example, he offered thanks for natural things in breaking bread and he hallowed the Father's name in the Lord's Prayer. He acknowledged his total dependence on the Father for his ministry and praised the Father for the revelation people needed.[20] He sang with his disciples and prayed with them and he offered intercession for other people and for future disciples.[21] He glorified the Father and blessed people in word and action. He loved the Father and obeyed him, so that his whole life was lived in honour and service for God.[22] He submitted his will to his Father in prayer and finally gave himself to him in total self-offering in his passion and death. All these things, along with teaching God's word and interpreting the Scriptures, Jesus offered to the Father through his whole life and death. They are integral aspects of what we call Christian worship. Whether we think of the offering of the lives of individuals in their whole lives, or the church at public worship, it consists of thanks, praise, blessing, prayer, music, glorifying and honouring God, and love for God expressed in obedience and self-sacrifice and in blessing others. These are the basic forms of Christian public worship. Jesus incarnated it all in his life, his suffering and his death, so that he made a perfect offering to the Father.

Into this perfect offering by the Son to the Father, anyone who seeks to worship is incorporated. Human beings in their frailty are able to worship through his strength. Sinful people in their guilty disobedience draw near through his perfect sacrifice for sin and find that their worship is acceptable. Created things, all of them, including created human beings, are able through him to offer themselves to God. This pattern of honour and praise and offering to the Father in Jesus' earthly life cannot be separated from the being of the eternal Son of God. The incarnate Christ cannot be separated from the eternal Word. Therefore there exists in all eternity a relationship of worship within the Godhead as the Son worships the Father. Yet his submission, honour and serving love imply no lesser status of his divine being, just as the glorifying love of the Father to the Son implies no reduction of the Father's status. Christ's worship of the Father originates in his very nature as the Son of God in the eternal being of the Trinity.

Here, then, in the nature of the Son of God, and consequently in action in his earthly life, we see the two fundamental dynamics of all worship: acknowledging God's worth simply because he is God and offering oneself in submission and sacrifice to God and to others in his name. There is a dimension of worship that is based on the very being of the worshipped and the worshipper. In Christ, this dimension is the Son in his eternal being glorifying and honouring the Father; in the human being, it is the created to the eternal creator. God is to be worshipped simply as God, as well as saving God.

Worship as created beings

The final step in this discussion is therefore an examination of the human nature of Jesus Christ. How can we view the worship of God by the created on the basis of createdness? There are three possible responses to this question: that such worship is invalid; that it is merely a preparatory stage; or that it is possible through Christ the Son of God who took up our human nature in its fullness in his incarnation.

The worship is invalid

Worship of the Creator on the basis of createdness may be judged not to be present in, and not relevant to, the liturgy or congregational worship of the church. The idea that corporate worship by the church may be seen as rising from the creature to the creator is said to be theologically invalid because worship is placed entirely within the context of the gospel and is only acceptable to God on the basis of redemption in Christ and his saving priestly ministry. In this view it is *theoretically possible* to worship God on the basis of creation, but it is *not in fact possible* outside of the saving work of Christ, or the work of the Spirit in the believer.[23] A person who is in ignorance of the gospel, or who as yet rejects Christ, is not in reality able to worship God at all. This may be possible for angels, but not for fallen human beings. Therefore anything that resembles the worship of God is false, being either idolatrous or irrelevant.

In Old Testament times, however, the worship of the true God was not knowingly Christ-centred or enabled, and was offered on the basis of the covenant love and redeeming activity of Yahweh and his provisions for worship. Such worship is rightly viewed as being through Christ, who is anticipated in the whole Jewish sacrificial system. So having no conscious knowledge of the gospel of Christ is not in itself a bar to valid worship; Christ is nevertheless the basis for such worship. It is possible to benefit from the work or ability of someone without consciously knowing about that person; you can be blessed by something without being aware of, or acknowledging, the source of the good. The fact that Christ is the basis of all true worship does not necessarily depend on a knowing connection between Christ and the worshipper. There may be true worship through Christ without complete knowledge of Christ. This seems to be the position of the Old Testament worshippers.

Some say that 'religion', meaning human achievement, ritual and tradition, is now rejected and the only ground for human response is found in God's own self-revelation in Jesus.[24] In one famous phrase, Jesus' coming means the 'abolition of religion'.[25] Under this approach, the material available for inclusion in corporate worship tends to diminish. In some versions of such worship the centrality of Christ so dominates the songs and prayers that the worship loses touch with the creator God. Or the Lord's Supper, rightly valued as the 'supreme expression of all worship',[26] becomes not just the centre, but the sum of the worship. If we see the whole of worship as rooted in the cross, this can easily obscure our view of the place and value of the relationship of the creature to the creator. In addition the human nature of Christ, with its power to affirm and to express the relationship of created humanity to God, fades from sight as his divine nature and saving power are emphasised. There is more to Christian worship than this. It is not adequate to exclude worship as the response of the creature to the creator simply because Christ became a humanbeing to save sinners.

The worship is a preparatory stage

In a second view worship of the creator by created beings may be regarded as merely a preparatory stage for unbelievers as they move towards the fulfilment of Christian worship. In this view such preparation is replaced once there is faith in Christ, so that worship by the creature of the creator is superseded by worship on the ground of redemption. In public worship, content emphasising the creator and his creation as a ground for praise is regarded as having a preparatory purpose and not a specific value in enabling the worship of the believers. The Roman Catholic position seems to settle here: salvation is to be found within the faith of the church and leads to true worship; the only true worship is the worship of the church, the glorification of God linked to the offering up of Christ in the Mass, and the basis of such worship is the incarnation, death and resurrection of Christ. There is consequently no place for any other way of viewing the process of corporate or, indeed, private, worship.

This leads in Catholic doctrine to the idea of 'preparation of the Spirit'. The Old Testament and the ministry of John the Baptist prepare for Jesus[27] and there is preparation of the individual by the Spirit for the gift of faith and entry to the church.[28] The doctrine of preparation therefore arises from the acceptance that the Holy Spirit is at work outside the church and its liturgy.[29] But the strongly asserted official position of the Roman Catholic Church is that the Spirit's function in the unbeliever is to do the work of preparation for the gift of faith. Then a person joins in the liturgy of the church and participates in the Mass where true worship takes place.[30]

This understanding seems to exclude the possibility that the Spirit enables worship of the true God in those who are outside the church. We are arguing here for a much more active and living role for the Spirit in the unbeliever in corporate worship and beyond the church. The key text for us at this point is 1 Corinthians 14:24–25, where 'an unbeliever or outsider' hears prophesying, bows down and 'worships God' in fulfilment of Isaiah 45:14. When Paul says here that unbelievers in the Christian meeting 'worship God', he may mean that Christian conversion has taken place. This is unlikely, however. He describes the impact of the prophesying as morally convicting, rather than evangelically persuasive: 'the secrets of the unbeliever's heart are disclosed'. Also, the general terms of Paul's phrases: 'worship God' (rather than Christ), declaring that 'God is really among you' (rather than that the Christian gospel is true), indicate that a first stage of response has been reached. The unbeliever acknowledges and confesses that God is present and that he, reflecting Isaiah 45, is the only God. The description of this incident from the life of the New Testament church, shows not only that God is genuinely encountered by unbelievers in the church at worship, but also that more is going on than mere 'preparation' for true worship and such people are included in the services.

Creation as a frame for all worship

So if we are to think of worship of the Creator neither as invalid outside of Christ, nor as merely preparation for true worship, how are we to view it? A third way is possible. Worship of the Creator by the creature is a frame by which response to God on the basis of redemption in Christ takes place. We are thinking here not of the frame of a painting, which has no great value in comparison with the work of art it surrounds, but rather of a 'framework', an internal substructure, like the internal support of a sculpture in which the frame is an integral part of the whole. Without it there would be no substance to the artwork, no means of upholding and appreciating the perfect finished object. In the act of Christian worship the vivid content of redemption is diminished without the framework of creation. In fact, it becomes impossible properly to represent the content without the frame. Creation and redemption are integral themes in corporate worship.

Worship as creatures needs to be an essential part, but nevertheless a distinct part, of Christian corporate worship. It needs to develop its own forms of expression separate from and additional to the redemptive themes of Christian liturgy. It is possible to see the liturgical celebration of redemption as greater than that of creation, but it is better to see these not as comparative, but as complementary aspects of corporate worship, neither of which can be separated from their Trinitarian theology within Christian worship. We deal with this discussion by thinking of the activity of Spirit in worship and then of the nature of Christ and in doing so seek a more precise theological justification than we have seen so far for the relationship of worship and creation.

The Holy Spirit in worship

In tracing the development of the doctrine of the Spirit we consistently find the conviction that the Spirit is present everywhere, not just in the church after Pentecost, or not just at work in the individual life of the Christian believer.[31] The implication of this almost universal understanding is that when there is a response of moral beings to God, ascribing honour and worth to the Creator, this must include the activity of the Spirit of God who is already present with them. The Orthodox churches see the Spirit as the 'perfecter' of creation and the same idea appears, although it is not stressed, in Roman doctrine.[32] The incarnation of the Son of God in the world and the presence of the Holy Spirit in God's creation are a 'double structuring' in the universe, so that always the Creator is present in affirming and saving relationship with his creation.[33] The contemporary concept of the 'integrity of creation' asserts that all things are held together in God. This idea depends on a doctrine of the Spirit, God's uncreated energy, alive in creation, within whom creation exists, and who strives for its redemption and perfection.[34]

To say that the Spirit is at work in all creation to lead it to the worship of God does not mean that nothing is added in specifically Christian and Christ-centred worship. But it does mean that any worship offered anywhere that is worship of a Creator and Lord of the universe, may be understood as assisted and enabled by the presence of the Spirit. It does not follow from this that all idol worship and the worship of other 'gods' are essentially the worship of the God and Father of our Lord Jesus Christ. The process of distinguishing between the activity of the Holy Spirit and that of 'other spirits' is very difficult and uncertain.[35] But simply because it is difficult to discern what is or is not true worship of the Creator is not a reason for denying the possibility of the Holy Spirit's presence to assist such worship.

To affirm the Holy Spirit's presence is not to deny that worship can be subverted into many kinds of inadequate forms and is in need of fuller revelation in Christ. In fact, we might say that all human expressions of worship are invariably inadequate. The point is not the inadequacy of the expressions, or of the beliefs that give rise to them, but whether it is possible to worship the Creator without conscious response to the revelation of God in the gospel of Christ.

The universal presence of the Spirit in creation indicates that all worship, overtly Christian or not, is in some way accompanied by God's action as the Spirit seeks to illuminate to the human mind the majesty and power of the Creator through the things he has made. Any response to such illumination or prompting could be 'misdirected', confusing a fascination about creation with the worship of God. But at a fundamental level the 'reorientation' of a person towards a creator God exists and is evident in many different cultures.[36] The Spirit may enable responses that can be called, even at a very simple level, worship.

If the Spirit is God bringing blessing to his creation and to human life, this is so for all beings and in particular for human beings as they begin to respond to God in worship. It is also often 'pre-conscious' as human beings interact at a deep level with the Spirit.[37] Thus worship by the creature in the light of creation may be viewed not as originating opposite to or apart from God, or as merely a response to God and his action, or as humanly empowered, but as one part of God's activity and movement, energised by the Spirit and enabled and mediated by Christ. Every ritual and liturgical practice may thus be response to the movement of the Spirit who is at work in and through all things. Every person who begins to worship a deity in any way, however limited or unformed the understanding of that deity, has already passed beyond mere thought about God to confession of God. The simple statement of Hebrews 11:6 expresses the same basic position: 'Whoever would approach him must believe that he exists and that he rewards those who seek him.'

The worship of the creature to the creator, offered on a basis of createdness, thus emerges as one element of worship of the triune God. Such worship is not separated from Christ and the Spirit because it is a relationship of worship that gains its fundamental structure from the movement of God in Christ the Word. Christ orders the whole creation in relation to God and ultimately redeems, or 'reorientates', both the natural and the human creation.[38] Such worship is also the activity of God the Spirit, who is ever present in creation and is the energy with which the worshipper cooperates in order even to begin any response of worship.

Christ in his 'createdness'

There is one final and vital aspect of the third way of viewing the relationship of worship and creation, and it rests firmly in the person of Christ. We concluded above that any worship of the creature to the creator on the basis of createdness cannot be outside of the being and activity of Christ since he is the mediator of all worship. Therefore we turn to interpret what the nature of Christ may mean for such mediation.

We are looking to see if worship on the basis of createdness is an essential element of worship through the mediation of Christ. The key question is how one who is the eternal and uncreated Son of the Father may be the mediator of worship for the creation and created human beings. Our interest is in the human nature of Jesus Christ as the mediator of the worship of all creation and of the human creation in particular. In Christian thought, however, Jesus is divine as well as human in one person and so the way in which the human and divine exist in him is important for our thinking. The manner in which this is conceived was summed up in the statement that emerged, after many decades of difficult debate, from the Council of Chalcedon in 451. It says that Jesus Christ is to be acknowledged,

> in two natures, without confusion, without change, without division, without separation; the distinction of the two natures being in no way abolished because of the union, but rather the characteristic property of each nature being preserved, and concurring into one person and one subsistence.[39]

This understanding of the person of Christ was generally accepted by the early church and later by the churches of the Reformation. But there was further thinking about this problem in order, in particular, to clarify the manner in which the human nature of Christ the incarnate Word is united with the divine nature. Pope Leo, even before the Council of Chalcedon, had indicated that in the incarnation, the human nature of Jesus Christ was added to the divine nature, which the eternal Word already possessed.[40] The basis for the union between the divine and human in Jesus was therefore increasingly understood to be located in his divine nature, not in the union itself, nor in the human nature. The human nature of the incarnate Word may thus be seen as not having a 'subsistence' of its own independent of the divine nature.[41] Rather, it is included, or drawn up, in the divine nature of the Word. The human nature of Jesus Christ is therefore dependent on the divine nature, but it is nevertheless fully present and truly human, as the definition of the Council of Chalcedon had made clear.[42]

The importance of this point for our discussion is the stress that is thus placed on the full and complete humanity that exists in Christ. His full humanity provides a theological foundation for the worship offered by the creature to the creator and is a model for the manner in which public worship may incorporate this dimension. Even more vital, through this understanding of the two natures of Christ, the manner in which the uncreated may be the mediator of the worship of created beings is demonstrated.

What is included, or drawn up, in the incarnation of the Word is human nature in its created fullness. Jesus' human nature in its 'creaturely' constitution is the same as ours. Our creaturely constitution was not changed by humanity's fall into sin, nor will it be changed by ultimate reconciliation, but rather it represents the possibility of reconciliation.[43] Christ's human body is 'in the likeness of sinful flesh',[44] but is united to the divine in Christ, so his whole being is free from the power of sin, and that is how he is able to redeem human flesh. The interest for our discussion is that his human nature in its fullness includes 'creatureliness', the basic constitution of human nature as created by God. We expressed it earlier in the term 'createdness'.

Karl Barth in a courageous phrase at one point goes so far as to speak of Jesus Christ as a creature, not in the same way as other human beings who are not by nature also divine, but 'like them, a human creature, as they are'.[45] For human beings this means being created distinct from the essence of God so that in our humanity we exist as separate beings from God. In addition, through our sinfulness we are now alien to him. In Jesus, however, the same human nature that he shares with every human being was taken up into his divine nature. It is therefore distinct from God in its creatureliness, although it is bound to his unique deity in the one person, Jesus Christ.[46]

We have already argued that the Son worships the Father and that this worship is not only as the incarnate Jesus, in service, obedience and self-offering, but that it exists within his eternal identity and continues as one dimension of the Trinitarian relations. Now we can also see that the human nature of Christ is taken up for ever into his divine nature through the incarnation. So the worship of the Son to the Father also contains within its perfection and breadth the worship of one who, through the presence of his human nature, worships God in 'createdness'. This creaturely constitution of Jesus, once joined to his divine nature cannot be removed or adapted. It is confirmed by the bodily resurrection and exaltation of Christ and becomes integral to the continuing worship and intercession that the Son offers the Father. It is therefore the means of mediation for all who worship as creatures, both within and beyond the church and in the whole natural world.

The church at worship offers praise and honour to God only in union with Christ's perfect offering to God, as all the main liturgical traditions have stressed. But just because worship is through Christ, that does not diminish it as honour offered to God as creator on the basis of createdness, rather Christ enables it. His human–divine nature, as we have explored it here, provides a basis for the proper inclusion of the doctrine of creation in Christian corporate worship.

First, the humanity of Jesus Christ himself gives substance to those parts of corporate worship that express the response of the creature to the creator, even when there is no specific mention of Christ. This also means that anyone who comes to worship on the basis of createdness, rather than with a complete understanding of the redemption that is in Christ, is not doing so in separation from him. Aunt Jane, with the cousins, is able to engage in genuine worship since her worship as a created being is already anticipated in the worship of Jesus the Son in his incarnate life. Even if he is unknown, Jesus is the mediator of her human response of worship in his own human and divine worship of the Father.

Second, wide inclusion of elements of the doctrine of creation within the content of services is essential. Human and created nature, taken up by Christ the Word in his incarnation and offered to the Father God, cannot be ignored in worship if it is truly to reflect the worship offered by Christ. It is his worship as one who took up, and still holds, created human nature in his divine nature that provides a theological connection between corporate worship and creation. Creation elements therefore must be present in corporate liturgy for worship of the church to be truly in Christ, truly Christian. The manner in which this may be applied in practice will be explored in the final chapter.

7

Story and Meeting – Structure in Worship

In public worship creation and redemption are permanent partners. They need to be held together. We have explored the human nature of Christ, who is the mediator of all worship, and have shown that his humanity, taken up and united to his divine nature, is the only means by which the worship of created beings may be offered to God. The public worship of the Christian church takes place primarily in the services that Christians attend each week. Such services should reflect Christ's perfect nature and need deliberately to incorporate the worshipful approach of the creature to the creator. This has a number of practical implications for those who lead or are responsible for services as well as for the attitudes of those attending them.

However, before we go on in the next chapter to look in detail at how all this might be worked out, a further matter needs to be considered. To place creation and redemption in proper partnership in public worship is to imply that there should be theological structure in services. It is only when leaders consciously frame the service or liturgy in a theological structure that the relationship of creation and redemption can be effectively worked out. Within such a structure the important matters we have been discussing can take their proper place: the acknowledgement of God as the sovereign Creator, praise for his good creation, the offering of human beings as his creatures, and responses that lead to the proper use of his gifts.

The two 'theologies' of public worship

We begin by emphasising again the fundamental theology of worship that underlies all Christian public worship and is the basic assumption of all we have been saying. To simplify this issue, we can ask the important question: What do Christian people go to church to do? After dismissing the more superficial answers that might be given, such as to keep in touch with friends, to get spiritually topped up, or to sing in the worship group, there are two basic responses that people give about their reasons for being at worship on Sundays.

The first set of answers revolves around the upward look to God himself: his praise, his adoration, his glory and honour. This, people will say, is what Sunday worship is all about; it is about God himself, in his sovereign majesty and grace, simply being praised by his people. Many psalms and standard hymns, often based on psalms, lead us in this direction. The congregation sings, 'Holy, holy, holy, Lord God almighty' and almost the whole hymn is about God, hardly a hint about the human condition or the way to relate to such a holy God – except by praise. Some contemporary songs also reflect the same attitude: 'Let's forget about ourselves and concentrate on him and worship him'; 'It's all about you, Jesus, it's not about me', and so on. This is not the whole story about what happens in church, however, nor the only reason why people return to public worship each week.

The second set of answers settles on the experiences people have, or the benefits that they gain, from services of public worship. People will answer that they get help from God through the sung worship times, or from the preaching, or that they feel close to God through prayer or times of healing. One phrase often used represents the centre of this set of answers: 'I go to church to meet God.'

So we find ourselves looking at two basic 'theologies' of worship. We can call one the theology of 'story', or liturgical narration, and the other the theology of 'meeting', or liturgical encounter. These are twined together in Christian worship. Under the first heading, Christians go to church to declare together the story of God and under the second, they go to church together in order to be changed as they meet God.

These two basic strands emerge in all theologies of corporate worship. For the Roman Catholic Church, for example, the purpose of public worship is 'the sanctification of humanity and the glorification of God', phrases used repeatedly in the documents from the Second Vatican Council.[1] This statement is adapted from Pius X who, in the early twentieth century, spoke of 'the general scope of the liturgy, which is the glory of God and the sanctification and edification of the faithful'.[2] In the Roman Catholic Mass the story of God is laid out before the people through the set liturgy. This is the liturgical narration. The 'canon of the Mass', or Eucharistic prayer, is the centre of the telling of the Christian story, which declares the grace of the creator God in Christ. The canon leads up to the moment of reception of the Eucharistic elements, which is the primary moment of 'meeting' God in the liturgy.[3] Here the liturgical encounter takes place within the context of the liturgical narration: the encounter needs the narration to give it meaning; the story comes to its fulfilment and becomes personal in the meeting.

To take an example from a tradition at the other end of the denominational scale, if you attend a Pentecostal service, you will be caught up into prayer and singing that is primarily focused on God, his glory and power, and on the person of Christ, who is the saviour of the world. The story of God is being expressed in exuberant praise, while other aspects of the service extend the narration through Bible readings, personal testimony and preaching. Within the God-directed praise (the story element), however, another strand is present. There is an expectation that God will meet the worshippers in the present in the same way that he met the people in the story that is being told of his actions in the past. This renewed meeting with God comes by the activity of the Spirit in the service[4] and is seen through spontaneous prayer or manifestations of spiritual gifts,[5] through inspiring preaching, and also directly upon individuals through 'signs and wonders', or healing miracles.[6] Again, the story underlies and enables the meeting: the liturgical encounter depends on the liturgical narration.

In fact, these two theological interpretations of the process of corporate worship function together in some way in most traditions, the notable exception being Quaker meetings where meeting with God by the Spirit means that all outward forms are regarded as 'hostile to the pure inwardness of Christian experience'.[7] The key to differences between different denominations lies not in the fact that either the story or the meeting element is ever entirely absent in their corporate worship, but that different emphasis is given to the one or the other in different traditions or, indeed, on any given occasion of corporate worship.

Story and meeting in the Old Testament

These same two aspects of corporate worship are present wherever Scripture touches on the subject of public worship, and especially in the texts used for such worship. In the book of Kings, when Solomon's amazing Temple is finished, he brings the Ark of the Covenant and has it placed in the central shrine. The ark itself, with the two tablets of stone inside it, physically represents and is a reminder of the story of the people of Israel, their deliverance from Egypt, God's covenant with them at Mount Sinai and the gift of the land. Then in his prayer Solomon recalls the Exodus and brings the story of the nation up to date. He quotes God's promises to David about the building of the Temple and speaks about the nation's future story in the light of the assurance that 'there shall not fail you a successor on the throne of Israel'.[8] But at the centre of all this is an extraordinary meeting of God and the nation, a renewed manifestation of his glory. When the ark is in place and the priests emerge from the inner sanctuary we are told, 'The house of the LORD was filled with a cloud, so that the priests could not stand to minister because of the cloud; for the glory of the Lord filled the house of God.'[9] The story of God was interrupted by meeting with God.

Story and meeting is the pattern of many of Israel's psalms. Sometimes the story of the nation is told, as in Psalm 80, where events of the history are narrated so as to echo a present national crisis. But a refrain, sung out three times in the psalm, calls for a new experience in the worship,

> Restore us, O God;
> let your face shine, that we may be saved.

(Psalm 80:3,7,19)

This 'shining of the face', or splendour of God in the midst of the worship, is a recurring theme in the psalms.[10] There is an expectation that God will appear in worship, that he will in his mercy be encountered as prayer and song and sacrifice are offered. Other psalms, such as Psalm 95, the Venite, begin with the joyful praise of God. His creative power and his covenant love are affirmed in the psalm and the good times of the nation's story are celebrated. Then, without introduction, a different word is spoken. God comes near to his worshippers and speaks appeal and warning; he says, 'Do not harden your hearts as you did in the bad times.' This is a serious encounter with God in the context of a joyful story told in worship.[11]

In other places individuals tell their own stories of trouble and faith, and painfully try to recall the character of God and his faithfulness, but in the midst of it all there is an expectation (not always fulfilled within an individual psalm, as in Psalm 70) that God will appear, or act in power, to meet the desperate one. So in Psalm 77 the psalmist moans and meditates in deep trouble, but then begins to 'call to mind the deeds of the LORD'. He recounts before God the tale of the nation's deliverance and this new meditation renews his experience of the faithful God, who seems to come to him during the prayer, so the worshipper is able to cry out, 'What god is so great as our God?'

Story and meeting in the New Testament

When we turn to the New Testament, we find there is very little to show of what was specifically said and done in Christian services and therefore there is sparse evidence of this double theology and activity of meeting and story. What does appear, however, indicates the same dual action in early Christian corporate worship. Four things are clearly mentioned as part of Christian corporate worship: eating the Lord's Supper with bread and cup in obedience to Jesus' command; the instruction to read Scripture and teach; the instruction to pray for everyone and those in authority; and the command to sing praise with one another.[12]

In the Corinthian church encounter with God by the Spirit through the *charismata* had become more important than the true story of God, which is shown to be the essential thread running through the Christian meeting. So Paul corrects this problem at the very start of his discussion. The apostle firmly points out that the Spirit will never move anyone to cry out, 'Let Jesus be cursed!' Truly Christian contributions in worship have at their heart the story of God in the gospel of Jesus, summed up in the Christian confession, 'Jesus is Lord!'[13] Paul's keynote for Christian worship is, 'Let everything be done for building up.' The minds of believers are to be instructed when they come together in meetings. In this way Paul establishes the importance of the story element of public worship. He tells the Christians in Corinth that they are to speak what builds others up in their faith, while he also acknowledges the power of the encounter with God in the Spirit.[14]

Laying out the truth of God in different ways in corporate worship was central in Paul's teaching.[15] So he instructs church pastors to attend to the public reading of Scripture, including his own letters of teaching. Teachers are to instruct people all the time in what he calls 'the word'.[16] 'The word' (the *logos*) is Paul's shorthand for the gospel truth about Jesus that he preached. It is a 'message' to be seen in its broadest terms. It is about Jesus' life, teaching, death and resurrection, but it also includes his pre-incarnate existence and his final return, and implications about the nature of God, his purposes among the nations and applications in discipleship, relationship and mission. Paul could hardly find stronger words, or reasons, to express the importance of this same instruction to the young pastor Timothy on this point. It is worth quoting it in full to get the force of it: 'In the presence of God and of Christ Jesus, who is to judge the living and the dead, and in view of his appearing and his kingdom, I solemnly urge you: proclaim the message (*logos*).'[17]

This is a central task for every pastor or church leader. Above all things, they are to proclaim the message, 'the word', of which the centre is Christ. Such teaching is to be done all the time, 'whether the time is favourable or unfavourable', not least when Christian believers are gathered together in meetings for corporate worship. The setting out of this story in teaching is a central aspect of the corporate worship of the church and without it there is no proper 'story' into which meeting with God in worship can fit.

Praise and preaching

Some have argued, on this basis, that the sermon should precede the people's response of praise and prayer in public worship. The argument runs: you cannot truly praise and honour a God about whom you have no information. Instruction in the truth about God leads to faith in God, therefore we tell them the truth first and true praise of God will follow. So such churches have begun their services with the preaching and followed it with the sung worship and praise. There is persuasive logic about this argument and practice. But the distinction between preaching and worship is to a large extent a false one, even though in common speech it is often convenient to distinguish the praise part of a service from the sermon part.

We have been arguing here that the laying out of the truth of the gospel is an essential part of corporate worship because truly Christian worship does not exist without the 'teaching' or story element. It is false to think of this aspect of the worship as restricted to the sermon, since the whole of the liturgy sets out to tell the story. As you stand in church on Sunday and 'proclaim the mighty acts of him who called you out of darkness into his marvellous light',[18] you should expect this proclamation to take place not just in the sermon, but in a variety of forms throughout the service. And as a consequence, you and your fellow worshippers are in a place where the deeds of God declared in the story may be experienced afresh in the present.

Word and sacrament

There is also a history of this discussion. In the early centuries of the Christian church there is evidence that public services began with the inclusive 'Mass of the catechumens'. This was a service for those not yet baptised 'centred on the ceremonial proclamation of the gospel' and designed for instruction in the gospel.[19] This service was followed by the exit of the catechumens, those seeking admission to the church, and then the 'Mass of the faithful' was conducted, a Eucharist exclusively for those baptised and faithful to Christ.[20]

But the inclusive first service, the 'service of the word' as it is often called today, was not and is not merely a sermon. It was psalm singing, substantial Bible readings, and hymns and much prayer, as well as teaching in the sermon. So in terms of what we do in church today there was 'worship', which laid out the story as fully as possible so as to enable responses of faith. We need to note that in this pattern the Eucharist follows the service of the word as the primary act of worship of the church. At this point there is a persuasive argument for such a basic division of public worship into the service of the word and the Communion service. Adoration of Christ and renewed meeting with Christ in the Communion service certainly need to be preceded, generally speaking, by the teaching. As Luther pointed out, everything in worship is a means of the blessing of God to the people, imparted through the gift of righteousness, which is first offered in the gospel word, so that the believer may 'hear' and believe in Christ, who is then displayed in the signs of the sacrament, so that the believer may 'use' and receive.[21] This fundamental pattern of 'word and sacrament' is used in almost all churches in our contexts today. As we have seen, it has both long historical precedent and firm theological logic.

Spirit and truth

The gospel story underlies all the New Testament letters so that whatever else might be expected to take place in supernatural encounter with God in church worship, the truth of Jesus is to be set out at the heart of it. When the story is laid out in praise of God in the course of the Christian meeting – a wide and glorious vision of the Son of God, the agent of creation, who shared the Father's glory, who came to redeem and who will return again to bring the universe to a great fulfilment – there can be an expectation that the Spirit of God will be at work among the people. The meeting with God takes place in the context of the story of God.

Jesus himself promised the unnamed woman at the well that because of his coming and work, worship is now 'in spirit and in truth'.[22] Here is the pivotal statement of the New Testament on the subject of worship from the very lips of Jesus. It is the summary of all we have been saying about worship as the conjunction of story and meeting. Jesus declares in this simple but profound statement that a new way of worship has begun; the whole of life may now be lived 'in spirit' because the God who is spirit has initiated a new way of meeting him, found in adoring honour of the one who is the 'truth'. When Christians are together for public worship, it is not a dead, inactive ritual, tied to one place or method, but a continual and repeated encounter with God in the spiritual realm. This is the essential nature of new life lived in union with Christ, and it is the nature of Christian public worship.

Meeting and story in conflict

It is at the junction of what we have called the 'two theologies' of public worship that tensions are created and often the fur flies in church life. A desire for more of one, or more of the other, in worship becomes the basis by which people judge the value of any particular service. Some assess the worth of a service of worship by the quality of the liturgical narration – how much doctrinal or gospel content there was in the liturgy. Others judge by the experience of the liturgical meeting and may say that they did not find the service helpful, by which they usually mean that it was not spiritually moving, or did not provide them with the sense of meeting with God that they longed for. This is often characterised during conflicts over worship in local churches as a call for 'hymns with proper content', or an opposing call for more 'spiritual worship songs'. In fact, the conflict is not to do with hymns or songs in themselves, but is the inevitable tension between the story element and the meeting element. As we have seen, either without the other is always inadequate. Emotional and personal responses to God based on little gospel content will always leave people unsatisfied. However, mere theologically acute words that do not seem to enable a meeting with God in the Spirit, or are dry and lacking personal engagement, will die by degrees. Neither is fully Christian worship.

Meeting and story in any style

We have tried to demonstrate that Christian corporate worship must be a recollection, recounting and enacting of the wonderful works of God and, in particular, of the story of redemption, during which a new encounter with God is both expected and offered. This is the underlying double theology of public worship and liturgy that is seen in all the main Christian traditions and is present in both Old Testament and New Testament where corporate worship is described. It is not a question of the style, or the manner, in which the story is told. In the history of the church the story has sometimes been recounted in formal style, set in carefully constructed liturgy, and at other times in informal ways, conveyed in spontaneous and free worship. In some forms of worship it is based on many spoken words and long teaching sermons, in others it has been expressed in songs and through spiritual gifts. But the story should be told clearly and broadly and opportunity given for response to it so the great story of the gospel becomes deeply connected with the lesser story of each worshipper and of that community of disciples.

Recovering the creation story

The narrative element of the worship cannot be simply the story of the human life of Jesus. His incarnation speaks of a divine life before his birth, an extension backwards that incorporates the creation of the world and of humankind. This is part of the liturgical narration. The content of public worship also extends the story forwards to include the consummation of the ages in Christ, who will gather up all things and deliver them to his Father in a perfect unity. A true understanding of the person of Christ and the gospel story will always do that. The Gospel of John begins with Christ as the mediator of creation and ends with 'until I come'.[23]

The great passages of praise in the New Testament place Christ in relationship to the creating work of the God and ruler of that creation. In Christian praise 'You are worthy, our Lord and God . . . for you created' is matched by 'Worthy is the Lamb that was slaughtered'.[24] The declaration is made that Christ is the one in whom 'all things in heaven and earth were created'[25] and that finally all created things will be 'under his feet'.[26] Christ is displayed not only as the means of human deliverance, but also as the original mediator of God's first act of creation, the present Lord and sustainer of it, and its ultimate ruler under God because of his redeeming work. There is no greater story than this.

Worship with the whole story

When a person who leads worship in any given service grasps and presents the theological structure of the narrative of Christ, how does it work out in practice? If you have that responsibility, or if you are a member of the congregation, what might you expect to be the result of thinking in this way about corporate worship?

The narrative of redemption includes wonder at the existence of the creator God, the holy, sovereign ruler of all things. It includes the value and beauty of human beings made in the image of God. It includes the sinfulness of humanity and each individual present and their need to seek forgiveness for real wrongdoing. It includes the eternal love of God for his world, a love poured out in the incarnation of the Son. It centres on Jesus' life, in which he perfectly revealed the Father, his teaching and miracles, his suffering and death for sinners, his resurrection, ascension and heavenly intercession. It moves to include his promised gift of the Spirit, his universal mission to make disciples and the providence and power of Christ over and at work in the church. It concludes with the expectation of death, or Christ's final return, with judgement and eternity to come and the final submission of all things to Christ as Lord. This is the fundamental narrative of the gospel of Christ that all the main worship traditions have laid out in their liturgies. It is not realistic to expect that every part of the narrative can be set out fully, or even appear specifically, but over the weeks, as Christian people gather regularly for worship, and to some extent in the course of any worship service, these are the themes that underpin all that is done and said and they will constantly be rehearsed.

Within this basic narrative theological structure the worshipper enters and finds a personal place. It is as if, as the story is told, at each point in the liturgy the gospel offer is being made afresh, connection is opened and the worshipper finds the narrative alive with the presence of God. Every scripture, psalm or word of exhortation in worship may come to each worshipper as God's current word. A prayer of penitence is a moment of deep engagement and gracious encounter. Prayers and songs of thanksgiving increase the vision of the power of the sovereign creator God to

the congregation and enable joyful response. Moments of adoration in hymn or song convey the holiness and mystery of God. In
all these, and in many other ways, the narrative of the God who
is revealed in Jesus Christ is made personal and powerful.

In the reception of the bread and wine in the Eucharist, as he
promised, Jesus is made known. In hearing and responding to
the sermon the God who speaks is heard. In the ministry of
prayer as the service concludes, the Spirit is powerfully at work
to heal and to renew. The story of Jesus is the story of the Father,
Son and Spirit, the creating, redeeming and ever present God.

In the next chapter we will explore in more detail some of these
specific elements of public worship, that is, the events of the
'liturgical meeting' that connect the worshipper with the 'liturgical story'. Before we do so, however, we need to return to the
larger theme of the doctrine of creation in public worship. How
is the double theology of story and meeting placed in the context
of the subject of creation in public worship?

Broader vision of the gospel

The basic argument of this book is that in public worship the
vision of the triune God as the creator, recognition of the createdness and dependence of human beings upon God, and a stress on
responsibility towards the world in which the Creator has placed
us, along with its value and destiny, are essential parts of the
story told in Christian public worship. We have also shown that
this aspect of the 'story of God' is consistently missing from services in many denominations. There is a need to consider how this
part of the story may be strengthened or recovered in worship
and inserted again in appropriate ways in our liturgies.

What so easily happens in worship is that the end and the
beginning of the story are chopped off, or are touched on so
briefly that they have little impact on the meaning of the worship.
This is understandable when the centre is the life, death and resurrection of Jesus. It is his coming that is the new and amazing
part of the story of grace and that so profoundly affects the
believing worshipper. But the centre of the story, the incarnation,
life and redeeming work of Christ the Son of God, makes its true
impact when placed within the vision of Christ as the one who is
the Son of the creator God, the one through whom all things exist

and in whom they will be brought together in unity at the end. The creating God and the redeeming God are one and the same. This is the true story of Christ that inspires the greatest praise and that changed the whole world. The beginning and the end of his story make electrifying sense of the middle, and need to be more consciously represented in the worship services of the church.

Deeper sight of Christ

To go further, it is not only the 'top and tail' of the story that need to be recovered. It is also the deeper layers of the vision of who Jesus actually is that need to be filled out in public worship. Already we have explored the wonder of the divine–human nature of the person of Christ and shown how it is his 'created' humanity, assumed, taken up into his divine nature in the act of incarnation, that provides the basis for human beings to be engaged in the worship of the Father, whether they are Christian believers or not yet believers.

In the history of the church, and in most contemporary worship, the object of praise is the Father together with the Son. Hymns and songs are sung to God as Father and also to Jesus who is 'Lord', who is envisaged as seated on the throne with God, offering grace and blessing from the Father, by the Spirit to the worshipping people. This is how the New Testament describes him and it is quite right that the believer and the whole church on earth should live in the light of his ascended glory and rule, and worship the Son together with the Father. The offering of worship is thus, in the words of the traditional and commonly used ascription of praise, 'Glory to the Father, and to the Son and to the Holy Spirit'. This doxology expresses and affirms the full deity of the Son and the Spirit within the Trinity, equally to be worshipped and praised with the Father.

There is, however, a different way of expressing the position of the Son of God in relation to the worshipping church, and this needs to be present in worship. Another, and perhaps even more ancient, version of this doxology expresses the worship of the church as 'Glory to the Father *through* the Son and in the Spirit'.[27] In other words, the Father is worshipped by means of the sacrificial offering of the Son to the Father, and the church still worships through his continuing present mediation.[28] The believer, together with the whole church, is joined by the Spirit to Christ and is able through him to offer all of created human life to the Father. This view of Christ's mediation draws into worship all the things that form our primary interest in this book: the natural world, the body, human abilities, daily work, frailty, dying and death. All this, all ordinary human life as part of God's glorious creation of which Christ is the full and perfect offering, is gathered up, redeemed and presented in true spiritual worship through him to the Father.

This is not a dimension that appears with consistent regularity in the corporate worship of many contemporary church services, as we have already demonstrated. The more that the deity of Christ is emphasised in public worship, his kingly rule in heaven presented and his divine blessings sought, then the more likely it is that his humanity with all these other rich dimensions will fade from view. This is exactly what appears to have happened in contemporary corporate worship, particularly in Reformed and evangelical churches and in charismatic worship of all denominations. In public worship today the vision of Jesus worshipped as the ascended, divine Lord needs to be balanced more clearly with the vision of Jesus as the priestly mediator, the one who both represents and enables the worship of created human beings. Without in any way losing the vision of the divine Christ as the object of worship, Christian worship can reassert the humanity of Christ in his mediation. This is the best way to recover the presence of the doctrine of creation in regular corporate worship. He is the one in whom all things are offered to the Father and he is the one in whom the created and the human find their proper places in services and liturgy. Then the created order, for which human beings have been made responsible under God, may be seen in its true light and changes of human attitude and behaviour may be enabled in the light of Christ, the true and perfect man.

In the light of all this, in the next chapters we explore some ways in which those responsible for worship and liturgy may adapt content and practice in order to incorporate wider and deeper dimensions of the doctrine of creation appropriately in public worship.

8

Putting the Frame in Place

In this chapter I offer some proposals on how the matters we have discussed may be worked out in contemporary Christian corporate worship. I have argued that, like the inner framework of a sculpture, Christian worship needs a consciously placed 'frame' of creation themes so that the fullness of the wonder of the redeeming God may be seen and so that true worship may take place. The frame, or substructure, is an integral part of the whole and without it there would be no substance, no way to uphold and appreciate, the content of the gospel narrative. The beginning and end of the story of God, his first act of creation and his final gathering up of the universe, are deeply connected to the whole gospel story and give inspiration for praise and devotion.

In addition to this breadth of narrative, there are depths about creation that are found only in the person of Jesus himself. He is not just to be regarded as the Son, the Saviour who came to redeem, but as the agent and sustainer of all creation, the one in whom human nature finds its perfection in his obedient worship of the Father. The incarnation, and thus the vision of Christ in his two natures as we have explored it, is the ultimate means of bringing creation and redemption together and is therefore the model of how that same relationship is to be expressed within corporate worship. What God has created is taken up into the one who is the means of its salvation and renewal. Creation cannot be disconnected from Christ in worship, nor should it be replaced by him, nor must it be confused with him. Creation themes can be present in corporate worship in such a way that they stand out in their own right, connected to the redeeming acts of God in Christ without losing their own distinctness as a source of praise.

For church leaders or pastors responsible for the worship of
the church, what does all this actually mean in practice? How do
we enable worship of the Creator on the basis of createdness in
the context of local church worship? In the next two chapters I
suggest some ways in which this approach can be worked out,
drawing on the previous discussion and also making connections
to the ten elements of the doctrine of creation, which we outlined
in Chapter 4. There is much to learn from long-standing ways of
including creation in worship and we draw upon these. We have
also looked at some of the radical new practices introduced by
churches and individuals who have adapted corporate worship
in the light of the ecological challenge. There are creative ideas
and new liturgical material available from these sources and
these may well serve to expand our vision. In this chapter the following six aspects of corporate worship are considered:

1. Praise of the transcendent Creator
2. Celebration of the humanity of Christ
3. Ecological penitence
4. The offering
5. Testimony to God in daily life
6. Intercession and petition

It is important to note before we begin that the following suggestions, as well as corresponding criticisms of current practice, are
not related to any particular style of worship. You may have your
preference for certain styles of praying, singing and organising
services. You may have carefully constructed theological reasons
for adopting and encouraging set liturgy, free charismatic worship or radical alternative worship. This discussion is not about
conflict over style, which can be discussed elsewhere. It is about
the more general point that theological structure, and in particular the presence of the doctrine of creation in its variety, is necessary for any kind of Christian corporate worship.

If you lead and plan public worship, you are responsible for
the choices, for the prayers, songs, overall structure, for all the
specific content. In church life today a number of different people
are often involved in this planning and leading. But whatever
process your particular church goes through to enable church

worship, the pastor, or the church leaders together, are ultimately responsible for what happens. In particular, they are responsible for the theological content of worship. For them to abandon this responsibility is a denial of their oversight and pastoral care for the people, since times of corporate worship are so influential in forming the spiritual life and the doctrinal understanding of the church. Whatever the style or mood of the worship in your church, the leaders have a prime duty to ensure that what happens is consonant with Christian doctrine and is spiritually and morally edifying. In the light of the concerns we have discussed, that must include ensuring a place for the worship of God as creator and a robust presence of the creation themes. Any church of any denomination or style can do that. This is the challenge of the suggestions offered here.

1. Praise of the transcendent Creator

The first and most important matter is to include in worship the praise of God as creator. This may seem such a basic issue that it needs no comment or additional attention at all. Is this not what we are doing all the time in our corporate worship? It is indeed. But there is neglect of the doctrine of creation at precisely this point and it results in a diminished vision of God and of the world as his creation. As I have already argued, this has arisen partly though the lack of considered theological structure in many forms of church worship and also because of an effort to sustain Christ-centred and devotional worship that focuses on the 'liturgical encounter' or 'meeting' aspect of corporate worship. The problem is less acute in formal liturgical worship, since theological structure is written into it. But more and more flexibility is now given to leaders to choose what they include or omit in such liturgies and so the problem applies even here.

In all the main liturgical traditions an emphasis on praise to the transcendent God occurs primarily, but not exclusively, in the opening minutes of a service. It is here that we could expect there to be praise of the Creator in a theological structure that begins with creation, the transcendence and sovereignty of God, and then moves to God's provision, grace and other more specifically redemption themes. In analysis of services for my own studies it is apparent that this movement of thought no longer takes place in many services. For 30 of the 91 transcripted services from various denominations I found no creation content at all in the opening period of the services under any criterion used for analysis. In other services only a single metaphor, or one line, offers some content about God as creator or a context of the natural world. So no opportunity is provided for worshippers to dwell on the creative majesty of God or his transcendent sovereignty over his universe. You may recognise your own church in the following example, which is based on my transcripts and reflects many services I have attended in recent years.

The leader begins by introducing the idea that 'it is good to be in God's presence' and the people are led into a devotional song, 'To be in your presence'. The service then continues with the leader inviting us to 'really focus on the Lord Jesus', using the song 'Jesus is the name we honour'. This song, happily for our purposes, contains the line, 'Let all creation stand and sing that Jesus is our God'. So just for a moment we see Christ as the object of the worship of all creation. However, there is little in the song that expands this truth, nor do the surrounding prayers and readings make any attempt to develop this thought.

In the opening part of the service, therefore, where it would most naturally belong, the vision of God as creator is entirely missing in favour of a vision of Christ. He is worshipped as redeemer and universal ruler and praised in his glory. This is entirely appropriate, of course. Praise of Christ in his glory is a central theme of Christian worship, in some ways its centre. But praise for the triune creator God should not be squeezed out, at this point in a service in particular, and replaced by other matters, however worthy and important. My proposal is that praise, particularly in the opening moments of a service, provides the best place for significant content about the doctrine of creation. It provides, at the start, a basic frame on which the whole content of corporate worship is built. There are several simple practical ways to avoid this common trap when preparing and leading worship.

The Bible

We can read the Bible aloud. In much evangelical or Pentecostal-style worship there is no Bible reading at all in the doxological part of the service (as opposed to readings attached to the teaching and preaching part).[1] This is a strange and unhealthy development when there are such rich resources in the Bible available for public worship. Reading the Scriptures publicly is one thing that the apostle Paul specifically instructs pastors to do.[2]

When Scripture is read out in the course of worship, as part of the worship, it brings a large and profound sense of God. Most passages of Scripture that are suitable for encouraging praise and worship include some reference to God the creator. One such passage might be read at the start as a traditional 'call to worship' or as an encouragement to praise, it may be inserted into or between opening songs, or it may form the beginning of a led prayer. The Old Testament prophets have many sections that speak of God's creative power, transcendence and rule over all things. The book of Job, for example, and Isaiah 40 to 43 contain images and metaphors from the natural world, placing God in sovereign relation to his creation. There are also some passages from the New Testament that are useful in this context. You could, for example, mine Ephesians 1, Hebrews 1 or Revelation 5–6 for such material. Most books of liturgy or public prayer provide examples of suitable Scripture.

The Psalms

The obvious way to use Scripture in the early part of a service, and it is well used in all standard liturgies, is to *read or sing psalms.* It is almost impossible to find a psalm of praise that does not set God in relation to his creation, and then to his human creation, in its turn, in a position of humble, thankful and joyful worship. If you want to encourage people to praise, read them a psalm. Read or sing a psalm of praise together and the people find themselves immediately set within creation, under God's good blessings and gracious covenant rule. Many psalms are set to music, in ancient or contemporary style. However it is done, you can use Scripture as a vehicle of praise that from the start sets the creator God in view.

Prayer

We can pray prayers of praise. The prayers at the beginning of a service should reflect the same spirit as that of the psalms of praise. If you are a pastor or leader of worship, the most creative and influential thing that you do in leading worship is to frame and utter the words of the prayers. If you use a set liturgy, then this is not so much the case, but in most churches the leader has the responsibility of representatively expressing the praise and prayer of the people. These are not personal prayers in the first person, but prayers on behalf of all present: 'We praise you together . . .' At the beginning of the service the one praying can help the whole congregation into worship and praise. It is my observation that people long for someone to lead them and to do it with faith and fervour. In prayer this means to place the emphasis on God, rather than on the needs and desires and condition of the congregation.

So often the opening moments of a contemporary service are taken up with prayer that calls on God to 'be with us', or says how 'wonderful it is to be in your presence' or how much 'we really want to worship you today'. There is a place for such expression, but if a leader of worship wishes to help people experience the presence of God and wonder at the grace of being able to worship him, the best way is not to talk about the wonder, but to talk about the God of the wonder, to express something of the nature of God and so lead others to enter that place of meeting in the Spirit. You do that by placing the focus on God himself in adoration, praise and thanks. Robust praise recites the deeds and character of God, his greatness and creative power, declares his love towards all he has made, and dwells on his holiness and mighty work for the renewal and saving of humanity and creation. What the people may be feeling and thinking about themselves and their worship will only find true perspective in the light of God, who is the object of the praise.

Hymns and songs

A similar point needs to be made about choices of songs and hymns. Leaders can *choose hymns or songs that focus on God*. There are many devotional hymns and songs; they express personal and intimate worship to God, or they focus on the person of Christ in his redeeming acts and on the presence of the Holy Spirit. These are all good in their place in corporate worship, but they are not usually the best way to begin a service. One reason for this arises out of the mission opportunity to those present who are not yet believers.

A further reason is equally important. Under any conception of a theological structure to worship, we should not begin with this kind of song. The God who is the Father of our Lord Jesus Christ and the creator of the world, and who has redeemed us by his mighty acts, needs in some measure to be in view so as to give meaning to any expressions of love and devotion. To do the opposite is theologically incoherent and produces a self-centred and weak kind of response.

It is by praising God together as creator and Lord, especially as a service begins, whether in song, hymn, prayer, or set liturgy, that we most simply set out his glorious works in creation. Praise is offered first to God himself as the object of worship. But as praise is uttered his creative majesty is laid out before those who worship, so they see God in his creative majesty, holiness and power before moving on to dwell on his love and saving grace. There can be no universal rules for this, of course, and there is a multitude of ways in which praise to God can be expressed. But if, as I have argued, the church needs to recover ground by affirming the Creator and his creation in worship, then praise, whether in psalm, song and prayer, or in liturgical form, is the simplest way to do so.

2. Celebration of the humanity of Christ

The central fact of the Christian faith is the incarnation of the Son of God, as declared in all the creeds, which affirm that the eternal Son of God became a man and that the man Jesus Christ was and is truly God. I have argued that the human nature of Christ provides us with the model of how creation and public worship are connected. His human nature taken up into his divine nature is the way that our worship – human, bodily, and incorporating all of human life, as well as that of all creation – is properly offered to the Father so that what we offer is taken up and accepted through his perfect offering and continuing priestly intercession.

My own study of church services has produced only modest evidence that contemporary public worship asserts and celebrates the incarnation, that is, the humanity and human life of Christ. The worship tends to be focused on the divine nature and the heavenly rule of Christ. Hymns or prayers about his earthly life are unusual exceptions. The references to the incarnation that do appear are nearly all in hymns or songs, or in brief phrases, such as Jesus being 'one of us', or 'living in our world'. The language tends to focus on Jesus identifying with our suffering, tears or pain, rather than affirming in him the value and blessing of created human life. In some churches and traditions this is an endemic problem. In one set of ten consecutive services that I analysed from one church there is only a single mention of the incarnation of Christ and that is in a hymn. More consistent mention of the incarnation appears where set liturgy is used, largely because it is stated in the recited creeds. The lines in these cases, however, are still very brief and no development of the thought occurs, either to emphasise the humanity of Christ or to stress his earthly life as representing creation and created human beings.

Include the 'story'

I want to make three suggestions at this point. First, that pastors and leaders should recall, in leading public worship, the importance of the 'story' element. The story of the birth, life, teaching, miracles and passion of Jesus provides the very centre of the biblical narrative. Not that we ignore other aspects of the extended story of God, but we are never to neglect this centre, the incarnation as well as the passion of Jesus. In prayers, in the choosing of readings, songs and hymns, and in the linking sentences that often accompany contemporary worship, the story of Jesus' life may be recalled and made an integral part of the service.

Read the Gospels

Second, the Gospels should regularly be read. To some extent, the criticism that present worship does not include the incarnation is corrected here, since the Gospels are often read in the teaching and preaching part of services. The deliberate inclusion of a reading from one of the Gospels inevitably presents a variety of images of Jesus' earthly life. He is seen at work, eating, walking, sitting in the hills of Galilee and speaking of the beauty of natural things around him, and these all present a vision of creation in connection with the incarnate Son. He is shown being human, as well as divine, and the consequence is that as the people offer praise through him to the Father, his earthly life and his humanity are kept in view along with his ascended glory.

Dwell on the human life of Jesus

Third, I suggest that the aspects of Christ's life that affirm human existence should be held together with those that show its pain and suffering. When Jesus' humanity is mentioned in public worship, it is usually to show that he identifies with human suffering and sin in order to redeem human beings. This is an essential doctrine to include in Christian worship. However, the most significant theological foundation for affirming the beauty, value and goodness of creation is the person and life of Christ, and the relationship between worship and creation is to be found in the humanity of Christ in his two natures. Public worship can therefore enhance understanding of the goodness of creation through a vision of the humanity of Christ as the one who participates fully in the created order and redeems it. Leaders can pray, read Scripture and create liturgy that does so.

The context of the church at worship today provides strong motivation for leaders to include more direct reference to the incarnation and the humanity of Christ. While still retaining in worship essential matters with regard to his deity and lordship, the humanity of Christ may be included in these three ways. Such practice in worship also enables a more direct relationship to be conceived between God and the environment. It places the believer in a better position to see the value and goodness of human life and provides points of resonance with those in the congregation who are not yet believers since it opens a perspective on Christ that is humanly meaningful.

3. Ecological penitence

The evidence of my studies shows that in church worship there is often no prayer of penitence. A simple consideration of my collected service transcripts shows that only half (45 of 91 services) include a specific opportunity for the congregation to confess their sins and be assured of forgiveness. This problem is also observed where written liturgical forms are not followed fully.[3] Public prayers of penitence, including absolution, have been a central aspect of all traditional liturgies. The people acknowledge their sinfulness in prayer and together find God's grace and forgiveness. The individual's response in a service, as well as the whole spirit of the worship, changes when penitence is expressed. Something very important is lacking when it is omitted. The appropriate place for such confession is towards the beginning of a service, although there are other places where such prayer can be included, such as before Communion.

With regard to the care of creation, the general absence of public penitence in contemporary services leaves no opportunity for the church to acknowledge human sin against God in abusing or not caring for the environment. While there is urgent need for 'a Great Turning' in our attitude to the environment,[4] anything that might be called 'ecological confession' has not yet appeared in most public worship today. The evidence of my transcripts shows that even in services where penitential liturgy is present, the prayers contain no acknowledgement of ecological sins. The overwhelming focus of these penitential prayers is personal and relational sin, or unbelief, thanklessness and lack of love towards God. The transcripts I have studied never refer to any sin against or abuse of the non-human world.

When a prayer of penitence is included, there is opportunity at this important point in a service for recognition of two of the main elements of the doctrine of creation outlined in Chapter 4: acknowledgement of the relationship of the human to the non-human creation and the spoiling of creation by sin. The inclusion of penitence in relation to creation is one way in which the understanding of human responsibility for creation may be encouraged. Such prayer also represents an opportunity to influence the ethical motivations and behaviour of the worshippers in regard to the environment since regular exposure to the challenge of such issues does change behaviour.

In the light of the importance of the ecological questions facing the world, public prayers of penitence that include ecological confession should regularly be incorporated into worship. Churches that employ written liturgy almost inevitably include penitential liturgy, such as when the Lord's Prayer is used, but the awareness of ecological sins occurs very infrequently. In recently written liturgy there is some movement to incorporate prayers of this kind, as demonstrated in the Church of England's *Common Worship*.[5] Harvest material and radical 'earth liturgies' also contain substantial opportunities for such confession. Harvest services, however, are inevitably annual celebrations, while the earth liturgies exist on the fringes of the church and are to a large extent regarded with suspicion, so their challenge is muted. An urgent need in the contemporary church is for regular inclusion in public worship of confession and specifically penitential material about the environment. These things should not be confined to once-a-year harvest festivals, or left to radical pressure groups.

I am not arguing here for set liturgy, or inevitable weekly inclusion of such prayers, since it is never possible to include everything worthy in any single service. But over time, regular reference to ecological sins, even one line or phrase added to a prayer of penitence, is possible and is urgently needed. The environmental conscience, attitude and behaviour of Christians can be influenced. Church and worship leaders might learn the concept of 'conscientisation' from the church in Zimbabwe and use it self-consciously in worship practice.[6] In liturgies developed by these African Independent Churches, church prophets act as guardians of the church and at the beginning of worship require confession of 'ecological sin' from the arriving congregation. These are sins such as tree felling, overgrazing and riverbank destruction, which in that context represent heinous acts of wrongdoing against the whole community.[7] Western Christians need to see ecological sins as equally destructive to the local and worldwide community. In the light of global environmental irresponsibility regular ecological penitence in worship is quite appropriate, and changes of behaviour can be brought about in many small matters. A powerful means of such change is through regular acknowledgement of our personal and societal sins in regard to environmental destruction.

4. The Offering

We have already noted that the third element of the doctrine of creation as we have outlined it – God as the sustainer and provider – is consistently and regularly present in contemporary public worship. This concept appears widely in hymns, prayers and Bible readings in all liturgical forms and services. It is worth making one particular proposal on this theme, however – the use of the offering prayer. In most churches there are public offerings of money (sometimes called 'the collection'). Four examples of informal offertory prayers, based on real prayers from my transcripts, illustrate the possible emphases behind the offering.

Harvest thanks

The first is what may be called the *harvest view* of the offering.

> Father, you are such a good God to us in so many, many ways and so for all that you provide for our physical well-being, we thank you. Lord, these things that you have given to us are only because of your great goodness. You have given either directly or through the abilities and talents that you have created in us in one way or another. And, Lord, we delight to be able to return to you just a small portion . . .

Here the prayer simply acknowledges the gifts of God in creation and in human life and offers back a part in thanksgiving for it all.

Stewardship

The second prayer illustrates what may be called the *stewardship view* of the offering.

> Father, we bring you this offering as a sign of all that you have entrusted to us. We pray that the money given today will be used wisely for your glory. We remember that all we have is on trust

from you, so help us also to use what we keep back, and all our possessions, in a way that pleases you . . .

Consecration

The third attitude is the emphasis on *consecration*, in which the worshippers making the offering are encouraged to see it as a visible part of the offering of their whole lives in dedication to God and his kingdom. The second prayer above continues,

> But, Lord, we also offer this our gift in the spirit of saying, 'Lord, we love you, and we give it to you because we love you', and so we lay it before you, with our whole lives . . .

Mission

The fourth attitude is the *missional emphasis*, where the offering is seen as a contribution to the evangelisation of the world or to the provision of help to the poor. So the same prayer continues,

> with the prayer that these gifts, and we the givers, may be used that others will hear of Jesus Christ and come to know and love him for themselves. Will you please accept and multiply these gifts, we ask, for this purpose.

The evidence of my studies shows that the stewardship, consecration and missional emphases predominate in contemporary offering prayers. My proposal is that at this moment in a service the first should feature more strongly than it does. The other three kinds of offering prayer can certainly be used, but there plenty of other opportunities for such prayers. An offering prayer should, at least regularly, include simple thanksgiving for God's provision of employment, money, food and other creation gifts. The moment of giving affirms that they are good, are acceptable through Christ as worship, and can be rejoiced over as they are. The consecration of the worshipper or the evangelical purpose of the church might enter alongside the thanks, but should not entirely replace it. The stewardship emphasis also may serve our theme, since here the worshippers can remind themselves of the human duty of stewardship for all God's gifts, including the creation environment in which he has placed them.

A further point can be made here about the distinctions that are often drawn between natural and spiritual gifts, the visible and invisible provision of God. There is a habit of speech in some worship contexts that compares natural gifts with spiritual gifts. So, for example, in acknowledging the crowning mercy of God in Christ, a leader may pray, 'Above all, we thank you for the gift of Christ . . .', and so on. But it is not helpful to compare natural with spiritual gifts in a way that diminishes the natural gifts or creates the impression that we are embarrassed to speak of them in the same breath.

The offering prayer is sometimes the unhappy victim of such comparison, the gifts we present to God being 'meagre', or 'nothing' in the light of 'your great gift of Christ and saving grace'. It is better to enhance with thanks, rather than to denigrate, the natural gifts of God. In psalms and other hymns of thanksgiving his gifts are valued along with the giver, who is worshipped in the light of them. His gifts of creation and his salvation are both the subject of praise. In Eucharistic prayers both creation and redemption are traditionally the objects of thanksgiving and celebration.[8] The church would do well to remember this and express it always in prayer.

5. Testimony to God in daily life

In Chapter 3 we discussed the serious issue of the relationship of public worship to the daily lives of Christians and we saw how easy it is for a separation to arise between them. The worlds of work, family, local community and politics are often ignored in worship. It was suggested that one simple remedy is the inclusion of personal testimony in a service. In some traditions testimony is a regular part of public worship. In listening to many services from different denominations the Salvation Army services stood out for me in this respect. Personal testimony was regularly included, followed up with praise in song, or prayer for the individual. As well as stories of conversion or spiritual restoration, the testimony might equally be of work relationships, of family issues, answers to prayer, or of an opportunity to serve in the community and of the joy it gave. What happens in such a testimony is that there is a demonstration of the presence of God in the daily life of the one giving testimony, that is, life beyond the church and in the community. There is no way that a service including such a story can remain disconnected from the normal world in which everyone lives.

The one danger of such testimony is that it can imply that God works only in the dramatic intervention, or sudden word of guidance, or by acts of deliverance, rather than also in the normal everyday matters of life. The extraordinary is certainly God's province, but so is the ordinary. Some of the best testimony I have heard of this kind is when a person is invited simply to speak publicly about the effect of God's presence in daily life, family, work or community relationships. Most of the time such accounts are not dramatic, but demonstrate the way that the Creator can be perceived as present and at work in and through his world and then through his people. In this way, expressed in testimony during public worship, and followed by prayer of thanks or intercession, work and ordinary life are shown to be deeply connected to the church at worship. Few present can ignore the implicit message that God is at work for them, too, in the ordinary things of daily life.

6. Intercession and petition

A similar discussion can be had about the place of public prayer in worship. If leaders encourage penitence about the matters of daily life, particularly over environmental issues, then the next step is to pray for change and the power to behave better. If leaders call for testimony about the presence of God in daily activity, then the logical extension is to pray for those activities. Public intercession (praying for others) and petition (praying for ourselves) have always been significant in all standard liturgies and are commanded and modelled in Scripture.[9]

Intercession

Intercession has been, and still is, well represented in public worship. In the light of the enormous needs of the world, of which the media make us aware hour by hour, intercession is a standard part of the worship in most churches. It is also integral to the search for justice in the world, which is deeply related to the environmental crisis since the poor are the first to suffer where there is disruption of the providential rhythms of creation. Churches are very imaginative today in finding forms for intercession. Formal liturgy, extempore prayer by a pastor, open prayer from the congregation, visual or acted prayer, group or silent prayer, are all in regular use.

Some argue that such intercession should be offered at other times in the life of the church and not in the public worship where it distracts from what are seen to be the main tasks of praise and preaching. But this is to create a false tension. All that the church does should be in some measure represented in public worship. So the intercession of the church should be included too, forming part of the fabric of the whole story of God in Christ that is being laid out in the worship. By public intercession the church joins the eternal, priestly intercession of Christ. In his continuing humanity and deity he prays for the church and pleads for the world, as he did on the cross, 'Father, forgive them.' The church breaks bread and pours out wine, the fruits of God's own creation, signifying the body and blood of Christ given to redeem his whole creation, and in doing so those present renew and join in intercession for his creation. These are reasons enough not to omit such intercession in public worship and to include within it prayer for the environment and about human care of it.

Petition

When we turn to petition, the record of the contemporary church is not so good. All public worship is a form of petition, as the authors of *The Book of Common Prayer* realised. The introductions to Morning Prayer and Evening Prayer give four good reasons for public worship, the last of which is 'when we assemble together . . . to ask those things which are requisite and necessary, as well for the body as the soul', and the prayers and collects regularly said are substantially of this kind. When Christians worship together it is to pray for themselves as well as for others. But public petition is to a large extent a neglected art in the contemporary church. How often do you go to church and find that someone, representatively, prays for you, your life, concerns, needs, battles and opportunities, or for your family, work and neighbourhood? In my own experience, and from the evidence of my transcripts, it happens very rarely. The art of public petition is to lead prayer in church in a way that draws in the people, specifies in a subtle way their own situation and gives voice to their desires and hopes. As the people are gathered, petition of this kind can be 'an episode in the groaning of creation, a stage on the person's journey of faith and an event in which God acts'.[10]

Both intercession and petition, given regular and proper place in public worship, can make and develop the connections of which we have been speaking, to work, to family, to ordinary life in its demanding variety. Also they may bring out in prayer the environmental concerns that people have and the efforts they are now beginning to make in response to the challenges of the ecological crisis. They give flesh to the basic cry of the believer, 'Thy kingdom come!' Such prayer brings creation and worship together in a very direct way.

In this chapter I have suggested some ways in which Sunday worship might be adapted to include aspects of the doctrine of creation. I have also argued for ways in which the ordinary lives of worshippers and their concerns over the environment might be more deliberately represented in worship. In the light of the current climate of interest and concern about environmental issues, and because the church has a fresh desire to connect worship and daily life, pastors and leaders have a serious responsibility deliberately to include content of such a kind. Praise of the Creator, the celebration of the humanity of Christ, penitence about ecological failure, better use of the offering, testimony of daily life, and strengthened intercession and petition are all possible of development in this direction. There are two further subjects of great interest to us, however, to which we now can turn.

9

Creation Thinking in Worship – Blessing and Metaphor

The last two practical proposals we consider are broader than those we looked at in the last chapter. They concern more general thinking about what is taking place in public worship and how aspects of the doctrine of creation are incorporated in services. I invite you to a shift in your thinking, first about the subject of God's blessing, and then about the use of metaphor in corporate worship and liturgy.

Blessing

The first of these issues may be approached by thinking about blessing in worship. We can think most obviously about the conclusion of services, what is often called the 'benediction'. This discussion also applies to other acts of blessing, such as at a wedding service and an infant dedication, or at other less frequent occasions, such as blessing a new home.

When you prepare or lead a service you need to have some idea about where and how you understand God to be active among the people both in the service itself and also in relation to their lives in general. A student of mine was asked by a keen sailor in the village to bless his new yacht down on the Solent. He told us this story to gain our insight about how he should respond. The student group had quite a discussion about whether this was an appropriate thing for a Christian minister to do. They wisely decided it was: that God's blessing extended to people's pleasures and possessions, and to non-Christians, although the blessing of God did not alter his call to generosity and good stewardship of his gifts. Blessing of this kind is directly to do with our understanding of creation in relation to acts of worship, whether in church or on the river.

Blessed and delivered

Blessing is 'an issue that lies off the beaten tracks' and it has, until quite recently, been ignored in biblical studies.[1] Blessings are pronounced in various occasions of public worship, and often at the end of Sunday services. They bring out the fourth element of the doctrine of creation as we have outlined it: that God is present in his creation and at work in it for good. For the Old Testament scholar Claus Westermann, blessing

> includes growth and maturity, the increase and decrease of powers, recovery and strengthening, hunger and plenty. Further, it means the person in the community, from marriage and the family to all the differentiations of community life, in his or her work, in economic life with all its problems.[2]

What Westermann means here is that we need to think of the blessing of God first upon the creation, on the natural processes of life, processes which he has arranged and which he sustains for all creation. We need to consider this creation blessing of God before we think of the saving interventions of God, or at least alongside of them. Salvation is not only being 'delivered', it is being 'blessed' with the ongoing results of that salvation. But God's blessing as described in Scripture is given not only to the chosen people, or to Christian believers, but also to the world he has made in its generality. The first blessing of God was placed upon 'every living creature', so that they would be fruitful and multiply and fill the earth. Then he also blessed the man and the woman, and through them all humanity, so that they would be fruitful and fill the earth and subdue it.[3] And all was declared to be good in his sight. God does not merely work in intervention and deliverance for some, but in blessing, in the constant quiet of presence and peace for all his creatures.[4]

Blessing from public worship

The concept of blessing seen and applied in this way is one profound means of developing broader understanding of the Creator and his creation in corporate worship. Blessing as the general affirmation by God of his world and as an expression of the joy that creation brings, draws us near to a vision of the creator God, his world and natural life in worship. Walter Brueggemann makes the connection between blessing in worship and the world about us when he says, 'It is understanding of blessing which offers a new way of thinking, both about liturgy and about secularisation. Indeed it may be the link between the two.'[5]

Blessing and creation are related specifically in corporate worship, and the practice of liturgical blessing introduces a connection between worship and creation, between God and the so-called 'secular' world of work, family and community. The early history of the tribes of Israel, after they had entered the land of Canaan, embodied, through their regular times of worship and feasts, a conviction about God's activity in daily life. '[The] flow of blessing to and from the sanctuary', said Westermann, 'was an essential part of the life of the Israelite farmer.'[6] The promise that 'seedtime and harvest will never cease'[7] is worked out in a rhythm of regular blessing, of going up to worship God and moving back to daily life. The celebration of creation in worship is a way by which each worshipper recognises that they live in God's world and look to him for his blessing on their life in all its parts. The experience of life and of God's work in it is so weighty that it can only come to its full expression in corporate worship.

The habit of weekly Christian worship and the regular feasts of the church are the simplest and most fundamental expressions of the desire for God's creation blessing upon life (quite apart from the inclusion in worship of the all-important specific Christological content or gospel promises). A regular sense of that blessing during worship is enabled by the inclusion of the aspects of the doctrine of creation that we have outlined. So when the minister or leader blesses the people at the end of a service, or if we bless one another, as is now common, what exactly is happening?

Liturgical blessing

We can tease out four different attitudes to this moment of blessing in a service and you can listen out at the end of the next Sunday service you attend and see which approach predominates.

The blessing of the Eucharist

The first, represented by the Roman Catholic view, is that blessing at the dismissal of the congregation is an extension of the blessing received in the Eucharist during the Mass because all God's actions in the world take their power from that sacrament. The Eucharist is the centre of the liturgy and therefore the blessing of God is ultimately to be found in Eucharistic worship. The Eucharist becomes the source of all the various kinds of church 'sacramental' blessings, such as the blessing of children, food and other material things. It also is the means of conveying the blessing of God to the world.[8] The explanation is well summed up in *Sacrosanctum Concilium*: 'From this source all sacraments and sacramentals draw their power.'[9] This view of God's blessing, however, may bring about a disconnection between worship and daily life. Since life can only be blessed through the Eucharist, the only way for life to be truly blessed is to leave the world and enter the church for worship in the Eucharist. The blessing given at the dismissal of the people is linked directly to the blessing of salvation and deliverance.

Evangelical appeal

The second attitude is to see final blessing in a service as an evangelical offer and appeal. This approach fits well with many evangelical churches and those with Pentecostal-style worship where the final moments of a service call people to respond to the preached word, or to walk the 'sawdust trail'. In this very commonly adopted method the final moments of a service are connected to the word that has been preached, and the final prayer may be considered as part of an evangelistic appeal. Or it is, in fact, a prayer of faith response, sometimes combined with an altar call. R.T. Kendall, formerly of Westminster Chapel, London, explains his approach in detail, saying to the congregation after preaching,

Jesus said, 'If you confess me before men I will confess you before my Father.' I am going to give you an opportunity to do precisely this in the next few moments. We are going to close this service with the singing of a hymn. During this hymn you may confess your faith by coming out to the front of the church . . . Your very coming will be a way of confessing Christ openly.[10]

The theology of worship underlying this very common practice is that the worship encourages and enables people to respond to the gospel word just delivered. Every service is thought of primarily as an opportunity for individual public response, if not for an evangelistic appeal. In many services the whole of the final part of the worship is directed to this end, with an emphasis on the immediacy of God's saving action. Any idea that blessing is general and may be extended into daily life is therefore absent at this point since the focus of the service is towards those who respond to the invitation. In this practice the object of blessing is also confined to certain individuals. Help is offered and expected for particular persons as the service concludes, and the process is designed to divide the congregation into those who respond and those who do not. This can be interpreted, and is seen in my experience, as a division between those who are to be blessed and those who are not. It easily results in the loss of a sense of blessing upon the whole people gathered.

Sometimes in current practice no general blessing of the congregation is given at all and services 'disintegrate', with people encouraged to respond to the word privately as music is played, and then to leave when they wish.[11] Clearly no leader will want to hinder such individual response, which is appropriate in its place and can be very significant for the individuals responding. There are valuable opportunities for this kind of ending in special services, or in conference and mission events. However, the practice of weekly blessing upon the Sunday congregation, and the profound theology of God's blessing that lies behind it, should be consistently upheld within worship as a whole.

Renewal and healing

Similar is the third attitude, in which the blessing offered is for holiness or healing. The emphasis is now on meeting with God in renewed spiritual encounter for the purpose of spiritual or physical healing, and for receiving power to witness or to live a holy life. The development of this attitude to blessing is most recently illustrated by the 1980s signs and wonders movement[12] and the 1990s 'Toronto' blessing.[13] My argument is not against offering healing or renewed blessing of the Spirit during corporate worship, which must be seen as part of the gospel. Nor am I here challenging the value of the contemporary practice of 'prayer ministry' at the end of corporate worship.[14] It is simply to note that these practices, when used to the exclusion of liturgical blessing, involve a serious omission, which has a long-term effect on the worshippers' understanding of blessing and their experience of God present in and at work in creation and daily life.

What about the rest?

There is no fundamental reason why blessing at dismissal should not be given in these three ways and each has its merits and place in public worship. Note, however, that each of these confines blessing to certain classes of people: those who receive the sacrament, those who respond to the gospel or those who offer themselves for prayer at the end of a service. What about the rest?

There is a fourth approach. I want to stress that the concept of blessing is wider than these first three approaches indicate. So the final moment of regular public worship, as well as other times in worship, might more profitably express that blessing. General blessing of all the people should not merely be swept aside in favour of a moment of evangelistic opportunity or revival encounter. Even if these ways of ending services are incorporated, the very last blessing of a service should be upon all the people, on believers and not-yet believers. And why not on happy pagans who have just wandered in, since the creator God is their God too? Liturgical blessing at the end of services, or upon other individuals in home, family or community contexts, is to be pronounced on behalf of the God who created all things and blessed them. It declares his intentions for the world as good and it offers productivity and fruitfulness in daily life. It affirms that God in his activity for his people and all his creatures sustains as well as intrudes, maintains as well as transforms.

Closest to this approach is the Eastern Orthodox theology of blessing in which connections are made to the world beyond the church and beyond the saving activity of God through the practice of blessing. Public worship in the Orthodox churches rehearses the glorious story of incarnation and redemption in Christ, but it also demonstrates and reflects the reality of God, his heaven, his earth and his dealings with it and its inhabitants. The whole of life is seen as holy, so that,

> In the immense cathedral which is the universe of God, every person, whether scholar or manual labourer, is called to act as the priest of his or her whole life – to take all that is human and turn it into an offering and a hymn of glory.[15]

The Orthodox liturgy therefore ends with a dismissal that is not only longer than blessings in other liturgies, but is also more open to the world beyond the church. In this blessing the activity of God as creator is declared in the daily lives of the worshippers. The dismissal includes the lines,

> O Lord, you bless those who bless you . . . Give peace to your world, to your priests, to our rulers, and to all your people. For every good gift and every perfect gift is from on high, coming down from you, the Father of lights; and to you we give glory, thanksgiving and worship, to the Father, Son and Holy Spirit, now and for ever, and to the ages of ages.
>
> (The Divine Liturgy)[16]

Here there is a sense of the heavenly pervading the earthly, the presence of God in the midst of the people and in the world, conveying his perfect gifts upon all. This is the essence of God's blessing on his creation.

Regular blessing during worship

Consistently including public blessing of this kind must produce a long-term effect on the worshippers' understanding of God's blessing on their natural lives and their experience of God present in and at work in creation and in daily life. A robust expression of the theology of blessing in services creates a pathway from worship to everything that believers encounter in ordinary life. In liturgical blessing a healthy transition is made from the context of worship to the created world in which everyone lives in the providential presence and under the good hand of God.

Regularly applied, the practice of blessing may also change the way that worshippers view the natural environment. Those influenced only by practices that stress intervention and deliverance, and not cooperation with creation as a place of God's presence, are less likely to behave in a positive way towards their environment.[17] A strong theology of God's blessing, together with the practice of liturgical blessing, conveying good into the daily life of worshippers, affirming their created status and stressing their responsibility, is one simple way by which the church can extend understanding of the doctrine of creation and influence ecological behaviour.

I am arguing that a sense of God's creation blessing upon the congregation should pervade public worship and be encouraged. It should lie behind all the regular moments of blessing upon people in the transitions of their lives. In particular, public blessing at dismissal should be regularly, if not always, given. It should unite, not divide, the congregation. Where times of prayer ministry are offered for those seeking specific help, these should be so arranged that they parallel, rather than subvert, the general blessing. Also, blessing should not merely recapitulate the saving work of God in Christ already expressed in the service through the Eucharist or the preaching of the word. While not ignoring the Christological and redemptive effect of worship, blessing should convey the wider affirmation of God upon the lives, homes and families of the whole congregation, both believers and others present.

The dismissal itself might be a combination of the New Testament or traditional blessings of the grace of Christ and the love of God, together with the kind of content represented by the Levitical blessing and all that it implies: 'The Lord bless you and keep you . . .'[18] The congregation may then go back to their homes not only with the knowledge of the grace available in union with Christ, but with a vision of God's general provision and confident of the fruitfulness, order and natural good that flows from their Creator for all of their lives, as pronounced in the blessing.

Creation metaphors in public worship

The final practical subject for our thinking is the subject of creation metaphor and imagery in public worship. As any Christian worship service begins, we are immediately plunged into a world of metaphor and image. The person leading may speak of God as 'king', of Christ as 'light', of the Spirit as 'wind', or read a psalm in which God is 'my rock'. A thousand other images and metaphors tumble out in our worship services in prayer, song and reading, and we give them little thought. This imagery is because the true and living God is ultimately a mystery beyond human conception. He is difficult to talk about. Perhaps it is impossible to talk about God without metaphor. People have always spoken of God in this way, as is shown in the earliest writings of the Old Testament. Jacob spoke of him as 'the God who has been my shepherd all my life to this day'.[19] In the songs of ancient Israel, God's nature is understood by his effect upon creation, so the song of Deborah says that when God moved

> the earth trembled,
> and the heavens poured,
> the heavens indeed poured water.
> The mountains quaked before the Lord, the One of Sinai.
>
> (Judges 5:4–5)

What is a metaphor?

When we read 'the Lord is my shepherd' or the pastor prays, 'Lord, you are our fortress, our strong tower', what is happening? A metaphor speaks about something less clearly understood (the Lord) as if it were something more easily understood (my shepherd). In the process something is added to the whole experience. A new perception occurs in the hearers about the thing that is spoken of, but they have to do some work in the listening process. The connection is not explained in detail, rather, the metaphor is offered to the people listening for them to interpret it and to fill out the meaning. So when you lead prayer or read the Bible on Sunday, it would be foolish to say, 'The Lord is my shepherd (not a real shepherd with actual sheep, of course, but he is caring and in charge and knows how to guide us through life).'

This only removes the power of the metaphor, which is that it creates a space between the concept of 'shepherd' and the concept of 'Lord' into which listeners are drawn and to which they actively respond.

This is exactly what we hope people will do in worship. We hope they will respond, not just physically with their ears or mentally with their minds, but with their whole beings to the God who is present and who offers himself to them in the process of the words spoken. We might think of the space between the metaphor and the naming of God as the place where Spirit meets spirit. The Holy Spirit, who inspires worship and makes it possible, acts along with the human response so as to make meeting with God a reality. This is what is happening in all aspects of Christian experience, of course, not just in the language of metaphor in public worship. But metaphors (and other related figures of speech) are of particular interest to us since they are so pervasive in the language of worship. They are also, on the whole, taken from natural things, the things of God's creation, and it is this aspect of the use of metaphor that makes a significant contribution to any discussion of the place of creation in worship.

So a metaphor creates a new possibility as it opens understanding in the worshipper and also expresses a mood in the worship. The metaphor is more accessible to people than a logical or careful descriptive statement and it gives a power to the occasion that it would not otherwise have.[20] Not that literal language is unnecessary, since both rational explanation and imaginative response are needed for there to be true Christian understanding.[21] We are thinking more seriously about Christian public worship today, because we recognise that people come to know things in ways that engage them as whole persons, as outlined in Chapter 1. The learning process, and consequently any changes in behaviour that we might hope for, are as much about the learner as about the teacher. There has to be 'engagement', response and commitment of some kind before learning really takes place and certainly before behaviour will change. The use of metaphor and longer verbal images is one way in which this process happens. It is 'a way of *knowing* not just a way of communicating'.[22] The words of Christian worship and liturgy are a primary vehicle for such communicating and knowing because worship takes place in a responsive and deeply connected atmosphere. The language of worship is a rich language for which very powerful images and metaphors are used. These words are not merely symbols and metaphors of something else, however, but because the one of whom they speak is the highest and most mysterious of beings, the living God, and because he is active as they are voiced and heard, they become the vehicles of his renewed revelation.[23]

Metaphors from creation

What has all this to do with creation themes in public worship? Simply that images and metaphors that we use for worship, in Scripture, hymn and prayer, are drawn primarily from the natural world. When metaphors are used, therefore, they almost inevitably create content that directly relates to creation. The substantial presence of metaphors of creation in my transcripts provides a strong impression of the created world and rescues many services from the danger of ignoring it altogether.[24] Creation metaphors enhance the sense of its goodness and value. They produce an awareness of the surrounding gifts of God and the beauty of what he has made, together with a vision of his creative power. This happens even where there is no direct reference to such aspects of God's character or his world. The idea, argued by some, that in public worship we should lose metaphors that do not relate to contemporary society, or replace them with linear, rational and abstract concepts, is short-sighted, let alone unworkable.[25] Rather, the church needs to reassert the value of metaphors and other images in worship and use them more effectively and wisely to assist the imagination and inward response of those who come through the doors on Sundays to worship God.

A metaphor of creation used in corporate worship is a vivid practical example of the application of the theological solution to the problem of the relationship of corporate worship to the doctrine of creation, as discussed in Chapter 6. I have argued that the doctrine of creation should be the framework of Christian worship, so that creation themes stand in their own right and creation is celebrated and taken up into the redeeming acts of God without losing its own distinct content. This is exactly a reflection of the proposed understanding of the two natures of Christ, who Paul Avis has called 'the ultimate metaphor'.[26] As Christ the eternal Son took on human flesh and became a part of the creation of God in order to reveal God and redeem all things, so the Spirit takes up the things we speak of from creation and places them in relation to God's eternal being and work. They then become a metaphor, a means of knowing and meeting God anew.

You might perhaps speak in prayer of the 'sunrise of God's renewal' upon the church, 'the flowing water of the Spirit' in the person who thirsts for God, or 'the feast of good things' that Christ gives to those who come to him. The subject from which the metaphor is formed has its own value and place as an object in creation and might be kept as a subject for meditation alone. Sunshine, clear water and good food are all gifts of creation to us from God, to be received and celebrated in their own right. In this context of prayer, however, each is offered and taken up into a new experience of God, an experience that we wish for all the worshippers so that they may see his love and saving presence in new ways and respond.

The range of metaphors

As you sit to prepare, or stand up to lead worship, you can have in your mind a range of possibilities that can help you to use metaphor better. Those who write set liturgy or songs and hymns have a particular responsibility in this matter since those words are to be used repeatedly. They should therefore have more careful treatment. What kind of metaphors and images are going to help us? The material for use in this respect is enormous and can be analysed into a number of archetype categories, most of which have some relationship to the created world.[27] I list the categories here with some comment about their practical use.

1. Characters or images of individuals with certain characteristics. The most notable and common image is father, mother and child, together with king, ruler and subject. Here we can also include shepherd, lover, bride and friend. It is important to note, however, that the title 'the Father (of our Lord Jesus Christ)' is not a metaphor of the

same kind as the family metaphor generally since 'Father' here is more a theological statement than an image of fatherly care, as is 'Son' in this context. Other items in this category would be friendship, citizenship and childhood.

2. The second is similar, but dwells on the qualities of the human relationships. This includes family relationships, which are often linked to the church or humanity. It also includes human crafts or processes, such as pottery, carpentry, agricultural work and so on. In these God is usually the one doing the making and human beings are the object of his creation. The latter may be regarded as having 'lower correspondence' than those of human relationships.[28]

3. Clothing. This is rarer in the Bible and in worship, but worshippers are quite used to being 'clothed in righteousness'.

4. Aspects and actions of the human body make up the fourth archetype. This is a very useful set of items in worship language since feet, hands, hearts, head, face, lips and so on all relate directly to the activity of worshipping God. In using these images we affirm the beauty and value of the human body and make a connection between the unseen God and the very physical nature of human life.

5. The fifth, food and feasting, regularly occurs, as does appetite, in many places in Scripture and in songs. The Eucharist, or Lord's Table, provides the essence and visible expression of this metaphor, which can be developed in words either at the table or at other times.

6. The sixth category is animals. We are used to images of lion, dove, eagle and lamb, from Scripture. This section illustrates one danger of imagery in worship, which is that to use very uncommon imagery in worship is counterproductive. So leaders and people praying tend instinctively to stay with biblical usage when it comes to metaphors for God. If you lead prayer to God as 'our great albatross roaming the seas' you would have to know your congregation well for it to work, and even then it would probably not help most of them to pray.

7. The seventh category is landscape or geographical features, which occur regularly. So we have mountain, valley, sea, rock, desert, woods and, most often of all, rivers or streams. These landscape images powerfully evoke a vision of the natural world and more creative use of them would be a benefit in corporate worship.

8. The eighth category of archetypes is the organic world of plants, the most frequent being trees. Sometimes these are images of fruitfulness or blessing, but can also be used of destruction or failure.

9. The ninth category is buildings, with which we may combine all human construction and artefacts. Anchor, city, gate, lamp, door, tower and banner are examples from Scripture and, of course, the 'rod and staff' of Psalm 23. This psalm illustrates how a basic metaphor can be developed using a number of additional visual elements. The shepherd and sheep idea leads to other related images, including the rod and staff, but also pasture, water, the table, the oil, the cup and the house. Such language connects worship to daily life by incorporating things that people work with or use in ordinary life, and in this way honours and values home and work in the created world, even when these are not the specific subjects of the prayer or hymn.

10. Under the tenth category of archetypes we have the inorganic world, such as sand, soil, jewels, gold and silver.

The final categories are water images and images from the forces of nature. These are the two largest categories and provide us with abundant material in worship.

11. Water images are multiplied through Scripture, Christian hymns and contemporary songs. So much so that water, river or stream, if used alone, cease to have much impact as images and, if over-used, entirely lose their connection with the physical world. We might refer to lines such as,

Flow river flow,
Flood the nations with love and mercy.[29]

Used frequently and briefly in liturgy, as in this example, this language has become simply shorthand for the activity of God or his Spirit. It is useful in that respect and certainly should not be abandoned, but its impact on any vision of water as a physical part of God's creation and consequently affirming its value and goodness is marginal. As well as being true of water, this also particularly applies to light, in the next category.

12. The final category for consideration is the archetype of the forces of nature. This includes metaphors of sun, rain, snow, wind, fire and storm. Most frequent in use is the image of light and brightness, sometimes related to dawn, morning or sunrise. Often, however, it is simply that God is light.

Developing a metaphor

A number of general concluding points need to be made here about metaphor and image. The first arises from the last two categories listed above. The image of water and the image of light are so widely used in the Christian context and have such varied applications in worship language that they have largely lost their natural meaning. The light in these phrases is the light of God, not natural light, and thus any connection with the created world has been replaced by the greater meaning. Thus they do not in themselves increase the creation content of the services, having largely lost that connotation. This process is well noted and it is at this point that 'liturgy comes into crisis' since it no longer has the power to enable spiritual response engendered by the imagination.[30] However, where the imagery is extended so that the picture formed in the hymn or prayer also includes other aspects of creation, the effect is very different and passages of this kind strongly convey an understanding of the goodness of creation and the value of the natural world, while at the same time enabling the vision or experience of a spiritual reality within the worship.

So there are ways that the creation connection can be retained more clearly. A metaphor, for example, is often taken up and combined with other images to give it a creation context. An example of this kind of development in worship is in the following Celtic style congregational prayer:

Be thou a bright flame before me,
be thou a guiding star above me,
be thou a smooth path below me,
be thou a kindly shepherd behind me,
today, tonight and for ever. Amen.[31]

This is what Jesus did in his discussion with the woman of Samaria at the side of the well. He developed the water image with her and in doing so gave it deeper application. We can show the same kind of extension of water images in a contemporary hymn based on Ezekiel 47:

Down the mountain the river flows,
And it brings refreshing wherever it goes.
Through the valleys and over the fields,
The river is rushing and the river is here.

The river of God is teeming with life,
And all who touch it can be revived.
And those who linger on this river's shore
Will come back thirsting for more of the Lord.[32]

The extension of the metaphor into such a strong visualisation produces a very different impression on the mind, with a picture of a literal river, valleys and fields that thus convey something of the goodness and beauty of creation, while the hymn serves its spiritual purpose. This approach provides one significant opportunity to include the doctrine of creation in worship. It is the responsibility of those who write liturgy or songs, and lead worship in whatever style, to use such metaphors creatively in order to help others in their worship.

Careful use of metaphors
Second, where human artefacts are used as metaphors, we need to recognise that they often convey a different mood or connection compared with metaphors taken from God's creation and are much less useful. In the mid-twentieth century when new hymns and songs were being written, there was a notion that we could use metaphors from the industrial and technological worlds in

songs and prayers. But this just does not work properly in liturgy. In prayer or worship songs we feel very strange if God is likened to a crane, or a tower block or a commuter train, or even if he is put into too close relationship with these things as we worship.[33] God is certainly interested in industry. He is present and at work in the urban sprawl and can appropriately be praised for these things. But they provide what are called 'lower order' metaphors. In leading others in worship we should find and use metaphors that enable a meeting with God that is sensitive and intimate. For this we need something immediate, not layers to dig through in order to make some connection. The correspondence is higher when metaphors are 'drawn from nature in her more beneficent guise' and lower in human crafts and industry.[34] Because of their human rather than divine creation, such metaphors draw attention not to God's immediate activity or person, but to the human experience engendered by the image, such as safety, understanding or celebration. Using images of those things that are God's direct creation is entirely different.

Unideal metaphors

A third point is that metaphors can use the 'unideal' as well as the 'ideal' world.[35] We tend to use the pleasant and wholesome things for our metaphors in worship: the calm sea, the glorious light, the green pastures. But fearful storm, raging torrent, earthquake and fire are also part of God's creation and the human experience of it. In a world where there is so much pain and distress these more difficult images would enhance the corporate intercession and penitence that are needed in this context. They also strengthen a perception of the threats that exist from creation. In a world of tsunamis, earthquakes and the more extreme weather of which we are now increasingly aware, such imagery in worship can work to engender greater responsibility and trust in the face of threats.

Bible metaphors

A fourth point concerns the use of the Bible, which is full of precisely the metaphorical material we are discussing. We have already noted the need for good use of the Bible in order to enable praise. We can hardly do better than to draw upon Scripture to incorporate more creation metaphors in worship.

James Mays discerns seven primary ways in which the Psalter incorporates the subject of creation. He notes that these expressions of the doctrine of creation are not, in fact, directly about creation, but are usually present to illuminate other matters, such as the display of God's rule over all things. Creation is therefore present in the Psalms in a variety of contexts in connection with other topics. In this way the psalms form a deeper and wider vision of creation and God's relationship to it.[36] Metaphors and images of creation that are set in the context of other subjects in the psalms provide a substructure that upholds many large themes.[37]

A good example of this latter approach is Psalm 1, where the subject is the value and power of the law of God in human life, but the means of expression includes the vivid simile 'like trees planted by streams of water'. This psalm exactly demonstrates the value of such linguistic practice in liturgy. The psalm has as its central theme the effect on a life of the law of God, but the memorable image left in the mind is of the natural world. The tree stands in its own right, but it illuminates and enables the connection to the higher matters of moral security and spiritual fruitfulness. And the whole idea stays with you.

Active participants

Metaphor in language is inevitable. In religious language, especially the language of worship, it is essential. It is also a substantial means by which we may enhance the incorporation of the doctrine of creation in public worship. The use of creation metaphors in the words we use in worship is exactly consonant with the manner in which God in Christ's incarnation has taken up the created order into his person. Metaphor has power to transform understanding in ways that other more direct and literal expressions do not. Metaphors of creation are therefore a significant instrument of change.

You might argue that metaphors and similes taken from the Bible are outdated and strange and are a hindrance to those outside the Christian faith who may be present in worship. However, those who lead and write can use them wisely and creatively. They can take up images of things that people see and know well, especially the higher order metaphors of the natural world, and through this language enable connection to the unseen God. As we have seen, this reflects what Christ himself has done in his incarnation, taking up human flesh and createdness and from within the world of humanity and creation calling for response. Metaphors call not for mere spectators, but active participants. The response we hope for in leading others in worship is not only of the mind and reason, but also engagement of the will and imagination so that every worshipper truly meets God.

I do not know if I have encouraged a shift in your thinking about the ways that we think about corporate worship. These two proposals – considering corporate worship as blessing as well as deliverance, and using creation metaphors – are fundamental ways in which those who prepare and lead public worship might adapt their approaches. Through the whole process of planning and leading worship, a sense of God's blessing on all things and a wise use of metaphors can instil a deeper sense of the created world, a broader vision of the Creator and a more responsible and thankful response from the worshippers as part of his creation.

10

Worshipping the Creator Every Week

There is one subject that has been largely missing from our discussion so far – the celebration of harvest. You might say it would have been better to begin our discussion with this theme than to end with it. The concept of harvest services, however, raises a basic point with which it is appropriate to finish: harvest services are occasional; worship in the dimension of creation should be regular. The practice of celebrating harvest also leads us to think about the relationship between occasions of public worship and the surrounding society, which is dependent on the harvest. In this final chapter, therefore, we look at the importance of regular weekly worship and revisit the significant issue of the mission opportunity that the church now has in this regard. These are substantial reasons for regular strengthened inclusion of the doctrine of creation in public worship.

Harvest worship

Annual harvest festivals are the most obvious way of incorporating the subject of creation and the natural world into public worship. The question of the place of harvest services also raises a fundamental practical issue, which lies at the heart of this book: that the celebration of creation in public worship belongs not on the edge of Christian worship, but as partner to the joy of redemption. The Christian God is the creator as well as the redeemer. We have considered that Jesus Christ participates in, and thus redeems, his creation. Therefore the worship of the creator God by his creatures, with the world he has made clearly in view, must be an integral element of the normal weekly services of the church and not be confined merely to special occasions or taken up by radical pressure groups for a particular style of worship.

In recent years some organisations and churches have revived a number of older liturgies that draw God into relationship with events, objects and seasons of daily life. Some are pastoral in intent; in these various transitions of life are blessed, enabling a sense of God and his activity in the ordinary, or sometimes painful, events of human experience, such as childbirth, miscarriage, coming of age, divorce and unemployment.[1] Agricultural times and seasons and country practices featured in many older liturgies and these are also now being revisited. In these services the sacredness and value of created things, and daily labour with them, are affirmed. One example is the reintroduction of Rogation Days, when, in past times, the planted crops used to be blessed, prayer was made for a good harvest and the community marked out the borders of the parish by 'beating the bounds'. *Common Worship* includes prayers for Rogation in both *Services and Prayers for the Church of England*, and in *Times and Seasons*.[2]

Plough Sunday has reappeared in response to interest in ecology or concern for rural and farming communities.[3] Resources for Plough Sunday from the Arthur Rank Foundation celebrate the work of the agricultural community. In these the goodness of God's gifts is acknowledged and the farmer seeks wisdom to work in harmony with the natural processes of growth.[4] Rich material of this kind is now included in the Church of England's *Common Worship: Times and Seasons*.[5] In some places ancient agricultural rites exist that seem always to have been part of the local church year. These include the rushbearing ceremony in Grasmere, Cumberland,[6] and well-dressing ceremonies in Derbyshire.[7] These events are taking on new meaning for the church in the present environmental challenge and might profitably be taken up and transformed by local churches.

In their traditional form harvest festivals have faded from the programme of many churches, especially in urban areas, or have been replaced by services about world poverty and justice. There has consequently been a decline in the provision of service material for such events.[8] The standard worship books of most denominations include material for harvest and other such special occasions, which can serve helpfully although it does not appear consistently.[9] Craig Millward argues for rejuvenation of harvest services as a way to refocus attention on creation and ecological concern.[10] Mark Greene calls for hymn writers to compose new material for harvest festivals in the context of a non-agricultural economy so as to make deeper connections between the God of provision and everyday work.[11]

It is a mistake, however, to think that reviving harvest festivals and other such occasional services will answer the fundamental problem we have been addressing and effectively respond to the ecological challenge. The theological points made earlier about the nature of Christ, in which the created is taken up into the divine, provides the pattern for incorporation of creation into public worship. There is need for a more integrated and consistent approach to creation themes in worship. Harvest services and Earth Day services held on Environment Day[12] or St Francis Day[13] are separated from the normal liturgy of the church and thus very easily lose their Christian foundations and authentic Christian theology.

The impression may also be conveyed from annual harvest days that these liturgies are the church's celebration of creation, which makes unnecessary the inclusion of creation content at other times. But although the two natures of the Son are distinct, they are united in his one person and offered to the Father. So creation and redemption should not be kept apart in worship, but each should take its own place and together provide mutual illumination as they are set in relationship to each other. Harvest and special occasions are excellent in their proper time, and are to be encouraged, but the primary means of celebrating creation and worshipping God as creator should be in the light of Christ during weekly Sunday Christian worship.

In the early years of the church Sunday worship was the celebration of creation as well as redemption, the use of the Christian 'sabbath' was not only for worship but for 'admiring the workmanship of God'.[14] Justin Martyr, writing in the second century, says that the Eucharist is offered on the 'eighth day', which is both the first day of creation and the day of the new creation, in order to 'thank God for having created the world' and for having delivered it through Christ.[15] For Irenaeus of Lyons, in the late second century, the Sabbath concept becomes a way of representing the final new creation, described by him in very physical terms.[16] Christian Sunday worship is about creation as well as redemption because the creation is being transformed by Christ, who is the centre and means of the worship.

In his 'ecological theology' Jürgen Moltmann concludes that the Sabbath idea is 'the true hallmark of every biblical, every Jewish, and also every Christian doctrine of creation'.[17] Sunday is the Christian day of worship since it celebrates the redeeming resurrection of Christ, but it also carries over elements that existed in the theology of the Jewish day of rest, marked out from the creation of the world, according to Genesis 2:2–3. The Jewish Sabbath honours creation quite apart from its human use or domination. It is a day blessed in order to affirm the existence of the whole creation before God. It makes all time holy and celebrates redemption since rest is the final end of God's deliverance.[18] The theology of the Sabbath includes a vision of a world both created and completed by God, existing in its own right before him, in which his presence dwells as he leads it on to be gathered up into his redeeming action in Christ.

Creation is not therefore excluded from 'sabbath' worship in the resurrection age of Christ. Creation is represented in it by Christ and is redeemed by his activity in it. Sunday worship draws into itself the biblical Sabbath concept in this way and the worship needs to contain words that express it. These are the words about God and his creation that we have been considering. They are to be part of the normal regular Sunday worship of the Christian church and need more robust inclusion.

Harvest and mission

To turn to a second concluding point, I want to revisit the idea that the inclusion of creation themes in public worship is a mission opportunity. In rural communities the evidence is that annual harvest festival services have always been very popular[19] and in some rural communities they draw more people than Easter services.[20] Harvest thanksgiving resonates deeply with the way that many people outside the church feel about the world, God and the environmental crisis. Even in a so-called secular society, and in face of the noises of the atheists, there is something that draws people to a place where they can acknowledge a god and his gifts in some way. Harvest, and by inference all creation themes, are therefore a missiological asset to the church. The inclusion of greater creation content in normal Sunday liturgy can therefore be considered an attraction to a wider section of the populace. The 'harvest' content of weekly worship could be more pervasive in the church rather than any focus on special days or festivals. This is not to argue against the practice of annual harvest festivals or other liturgies of this kind. The method that Israel eventually settled upon was perhaps the right one: Sabbath as a joyful weekly feast incorporating both creation and covenant, then regular festivals with their content rooted in both agricultural and redemption themes. The contemporary church, in view of the relentless rise of interest in the natural world and deepening concern over the environment both locally and globally, may wisely follow this pattern. While celebrating the regular feasts, including harvest festival, we can enhance the worship of God as creator and celebrate his created world in Sunday corporate worship.

The worship of the Creator for his creation provides a bridge over which not-yet believers may come into the context of Christ, may begin to see the presence of God in their lives and to seek him more deeply. In particular, in a world of ecological concern, new compassion for living things and hope for a better way, they may see our God and his saving activity for creation as the true motivation for and answer to their concern.[21]

In almost the whole of previous Christian history there has been a broad context of belief in God and his providence. Until about the last hundred years in Europe, a person writing liturgy and hymns, or leading worship, was working within 'a sacralized universe'.[22] The assumed context for the vast majority of people was a God able to sustain and to intervene in his creation. Today general belief in a Creator and his providence and gifts cannot be assumed and needs to be made specific on public occasions. This insight alone challenges some of the more devotional, evangelical or penitential ways of beginning worship and invites us to restructure our whole worship in the ways I have been suggesting.

Weekly worship is the 'shop front' of the church. The leaders of the church should make sure that they set out the window properly. One of the essential ingredients is to place right there in the window a vision of a God who made everyone and everything. This is the creator God whom, if they have even the minutest spark of faith, every person acknowledges and thanks as they come into public worship. More important, the relationship of the two great works of God, creation and redemption, cannot be found unless both are properly represented. The substructure and inner frame of worship is the creating work of the triune God. The crowning and final display is to be his redeeming work. But both are needed.

I have argued for the development of a new attitude to creation themes in worship by worshippers, leaders and those who frame worship resources. I have suggested new practices that incorporate the doctrine of creation more deliberately into the weekly public worship of the church. Such change is spiritually enriching as in worship people have a larger vision of God and of the incarnate Son who entered and redeemed his creation. This change is necessary for disciples who want to discover God involved more deeply in daily life. It is urgently needed as one Christian answer to the environmental crisis that threatens the whole of humanity. Above all, since there is no other God than the majestic Creator who loved and redeemed the world through Christ, there is no greater privilege and joy than to worship him more fully and to enable others to do so too.

Bibliography

Worship and liturgical material

Arthur Rank Centre, *Worship Materials*, <www.arthurrankcentre.org.uk>.

Baptist Union, *Patterns and Prayers for Christian Worship* (Oxford: Oxford University Press, 1991).

Church of England, *The Alternative Service Book* (London: Collins, 1980).

Church of England, *The Book of Common Prayer: From the Original Manuscript* (London: Eyre and Spottiswood, 1892).

Church of England, *Common Worship: Services and Prayers for the Church of England* (London: Church House Publishing, 2000).

Church of England Liturgical Commission, *An Order for Holy Communion: Alternative Services: Series 2* (London: Cambridge University Press, 1967).

Church of England Liturgical Commission, *An Order for Holy Communion: Alternative Services: Series 3* (Cambridge: Cambridge University Press, 1973).

Church of Scotland Panel on Worship, *Book of Common Order of the Church of Scotland* (Edinburgh: St Andrew Press, 1996).

Congregational Union, *A Manual for Ministers* (London: Independent Press, 1936).

Cotter, J., *Prayer at Night: A Book for the Darkness* (Sheffield: Cairns, 1988).

Earth Ministry, *Earth Day Opening Prayer* (Seattle University Earth Day, 1997), <www.earthministry.org>.

FARM-Africa, *Harvest Prayers* (London: FARM-Africa, 9–10 Southampton Place, London, WC1A 2EA, 2003).

Greek Orthodox Church, *The Divine Liturgy of our father among the saints John Chrysostom: The Greek text together with a translation into English* (Oxford: Oxford University Press, 1995).

Iona Community, *Iona Abbey Worship Book* (Glasgow: Wild Goose Publications, 2001).

Iona Community, *A Wee Worship Book* (Glasgow: Wild Goose Publications, 1989).

Krum, K. and H.L. Antolini, *An Environmental Stations of the Cross* (St Brendan the Navigator Episcopal Church, Stonington, Maine, 4 April 1994), <www.earthministry.org>.

Lloyd, O., 'The Rushbearers' Hymn' (1835), (Grasmere: Sam Read, undated).

Methodist Church, *Our Common Ground* (Harvest Pack 2004), (London:Methodist Relief and Development Fund, 2004).

Methodist Church, *The Methodist Worship Book* (Peterborough: Methodist Publishing House, 1999).

Murray, P. (ed.), *The Deer's Cry: A Treasury of Irish Religious Verse* (Dublin:Four Courts Press, 1986).

National Council of Churches, *Earth Day Sunday*, web-based liturgical resources 2001–2004 (Environmental Justice Resource Distribution Center, P.O. Box 968, Elkhart, Indiana).

North American Conference on Religion and Ecology, *Interfaith Declarations and Worship Observance Resources* (The North American Conference on Religion and Ecology, 5 Thomas Circle, N.W., Washington, D.C., 2005), <www.webofcreation.org>.

Payne, E.A. and S.F. Winward, *Orders and Prayers for Church Worship: A Manual for Ministers* (London: The Baptist Union, 1960).

Presbyterian Church of the USA, *Book of Common Worship: Prepared by the Theology and Worship Ministry Unit for the Presbyterian Church (U.S.A.) and the Cumberland Presbyterian Church* (Louisville: Westminster John Knox, 1993).

Raine, A. and J.T. Skinner, *Celtic Daily Prayer: A Northumbrian Office* (London: Marshall Pickering, 1994).

Robinson, J., *Celebration: Grail Liturgy* (Tywyn, Gwynedd: Grail Retreat, 2000).

Robson, P.A., *A Celtic Liturgy* (London: SPCK, 2008).

Roman Catholic Church, *The Missal: In Latin and English* (London: Burns, Oates & Washbourne, 1949).

Roman Catholic Church, *Missalettes* (John F. Neale Publishing, Mulberry House, Court Hill, Rous Lench, Worcester, WR11 4UJ).

Roman Catholic Church, *The Sunday Missal: Sunday Masses for the entire three-year cycle complete in one volume, together with extracts from the sacramental rites and from The Divine Office* (London: CollinsLiturgical, 1984).

Roman Catholic Church, *The Weekday Missal* (London: Collins-Liturgical, 1982).

Rothschild, S. and S. Sheridan, *Taking up the Timbrel: The Challenge of Creating Ritual for Jewish Women Today* (London: SCM, 2000).

Simpson, R., *Celtic Worship through the Year: Prayers, Readings and Creative Activities for Ordinary Days and Saints' Days* (London: Hodder & Stoughton, 1997).

Staffordshire Seven, *Seasonal Worship from the Countryside* (London: SPCK, 2003).

Thompson, B., *Liturgies of the Western Church* (New York: Collins World, 1961).

United Reformed Church, *The United Reformed Church Service Book* (Oxford: Oxford University Press, 1989).

United Reformed Church, *Worship for the United Reformed Church* (London: United Reformed Church, 2003).

Web of Creation, *Sample Liturgies* <www.webofcreation.org/Worship/resources.htm>.

General

Albrecht, D., *Rites in the Spirit: A Ritual Approach to Pentecostal and Charismatic Spirituality* (Sheffield: Sheffield Academic Press, 1999).

Allmen, J.J. von, *Worship: Its Theology and Practice* (London: Lutterworth Press, 1965).

Anderson, A.H. and W.J. Hollenweger (eds), *Pentecostals after a Century: Global Perspectives on a Movement in Transition* (Sheffield: Sheffield Academic Press, 1999).

Aquinas, Thomas, *Summa Theologica*, trs Fathers of the English Dominican Province, (New York: Benziger Bros., 1947–8).

Archbishops' Commission on Church Music, *In Tune with Heaven* (London: Church House Publishing, 1992).

Augustine, *The Works of Saint Augustine*, eds J. Rotell and E. Hill (New York: New City Press, 1991).

Avis, P., *God and the Creative Imagination: Metaphor, Symbol and Myth in Religion and Theology* (London: Routledge, 1999).

Bailey, E., *Implicit Religion: An Introduction* (London: Middlesex University Press, 1998).

Baker, J., D. Gay with J. Brown, *Alternative Worship* (London: SPCK, 2003).

Banks, R., *Faith Goes to Work: Reflections from the Marketplace* (New York: Alban Institute, 1993).

Barna, G., *The Barna Report: What Americans Believe* (Ventura, Calif.: Regal, 1991).

Barna, G., *Virtual America: The Barna Report 1994–95, What Every Church Leader Needs to Know About Ministering in an Age of Spiritual, Cultural and Technological Revolution* (Ventura, Calif.: Regal Books, 1995).

Barth, K., *Church Dogmatics* (Edinburgh: T&T Clark, 1975).

Barth, K., *Unterricht in der christlichen Religion* (Zurich: Theologischer Verlad, 1990), *The Göttingen Dogmatics, Instruction in the Christian Religion*, trs V H. Reiffen and G.W. Bromiley, vol. 1 (Grand Rapids: Eerdmans, 1991).

Basil the Great, *The Book of Saint Basil on the Spirit* (Crestwood, N.Y.: St. Vladimir's Seminary Press, 1988).

Berry, R.J., *God's Book of Works: The Nature and Theology of Nature* (Edinburgh: T&T Clark, 2003).

Bevans, S.B., *Models of Contextual Theology* (New York: Orbis, 1992).

Bradley, I., *Celtic Christianity* (Edinburgh: Edinburgh University Press, 1999).

Bradley, I., *The Celtic Way* (London: Darton, Longman & Todd, 1993).

Bradley, I., *Colonies of Heaven: Celtic Models for Today's Church* (London: Darton, Longman & Todd, 2000).

Brockelman, P., *Cosmology and Creation: The Spiritual Significance of Contemporary Cosmology* (Oxford: OUP, 1999).

Brookfield, H.C. and L. Doube, *Global Change: The Human Dimension* (Canberra: Academy of the Social Sciences, Australian National University, 1990).

Brown, W.P. and S.D. McBride Jr. (eds), *God Who Creates: Essays in Honor of W. Sibley Towner* (Grand Rapids: Eerdmans, 2000).

Bruce, F.F., *The Epistle to the Hebrews* (London: Marshall, Morgan & Scott, 1964).

Brueggemann, W., *Theology of the Old Testament* (Philadelphia: Fortress Press, 1997).

Burgess, S.M. and E.M. van der Maas (eds), *The New International Dictionary of Pentecostal and Charismatic Movements* (Grand Rapids: Zondervan, 2002).

Caird, G.B., *The Language and Imagery of the Bible* (London: Duckworth, 1980).

Calvin, J., 'The necessity of reforming the church' in *Tracts Relating to the Reformation*, tr. Beveridge, H., vol. 1 (Edinburgh: Calvin Translation Society, 1844).

Calvin, J., *Institutes of the Christian Religion*, tr. J. H. Beveridge (London: James Clarke, 1957).

Carmichael, A. and J. MacInnes, *Charms of the Gaels: Hymns and incantations: with illustrative notes on words, rites and customs, dying and obsolete; orally collected in the Highlands and islands of Scotland by Alexander Carmichael; presented by John MacInnes (Carmina Gadelica)* (Edinburgh: Floris Books, 1992).

Carson, D.A. (ed.), *Worship – Adoration and Action* (Milton Keynes: Paternoster, 1993).

Carson, D.A. (ed.), M. Ashton, R.K. Hughes, T.J. Keller, *Worship by the Book* (Grand Rapids: Zondervan, 2002).

Christian, R., *Well-dressing in Derbyshire* (Derby: Derbyshire Countryside, 1998).

Chung, P., *Spirituality and Social Ethics in John Calvin: A Pneumato-logical Perspective* (Lanham: University Press of America, 2000).

Clendenin, D.B., *Eastern Orthodox Christianity: A Western Perspective* (Grand Rapids: Baker Academic, 1994, 2003).

Clendenin, D. (ed.), *Eastern Orthodox Theology: A Contemporary Reader* (Grand Rapids: Baker Academic, 1995, 2003).

Colwell, J. (ed.), *Called to One Hope: Perspectives on the Life to Come* (Carlisle: Paternoster, 2001).

Colwell, J., *The Rhythm of Doctrine: A Liturgical Sketch of Christian Faith and Faithfulness* (Milton Keynes: Paternoster, 2007).

Cox, H.G., *The Secular City: Secularization and Urbanization in Theological Perspective* (London: SCM, 1965).

Craig-Wild, P., *Tools for Transformation: Making Worship Work* (London: Darton, Longman & Todd, 2002).

Daneel, M.L., *African Earthkeepers, vol. 1: Interfaith Mission in Earth-Care* (Pretoria: University of South Africa, 1998).

Daneel, M.L., *African Earthkeepers, vol. 2: Environmental Mission and Liberation in Christian Perspective* (Pretoria: University of South Africa, 1999).

Davies, D., C. Watkins and M. Winter, *Church and Religion in Rural England* (Edinburgh: T&T Clark, 1991).

Davies, J. (ed.), *A New Dictionary of Liturgy and Worship* (London: SCM, 1986).

Draper, B. and K. Draper, *Refreshing Worship* (Oxford: The Bible Reading Fellowship, 2000).

Ellis, C., *Baptist Worship Today: A report of two worship surveys undertaken by the Doctrine and Worship Committee of the Baptist Union of Great Britain* (Didcot: The Baptist Union of Great Britain, 1999).

Ellis, C., *Gathering: A Theology and Spirituality of Worship in Free Church Tradition* (London: SCM, 2004).

Evagrios of Pontus, *The Praktikos: Chapters on Prayer,* tr. J. Bamberger (Spencer, Mass.: Cistercian Publications, 1970).

Fairbairn, D., *Eastern Orthodoxy through Western Eyes* (Louisville and London: Westminster John Knox, 2002).

Fenwick, J.R.K., *The Eastern Orthodox Liturgy* (Nottingham: Grove Books, 1978).

Flannery, A., *Vatican Council II: The Conciliar and Post-Conciliar Documents* (Grand Rapids: Eerdmans, 1975).

Forrester, D.B., I. McDonald and G. Tellini, *Encounter with God: An Introduction to Christian Worship and Practice* (Edinburgh: T&T Clark, 1983).

Fox, M., *The Coming of the Cosmic Christ: The Healing of Mother Earth and the Birth of a Global Renaissance* (San Francisco and London: Harper & Row, 1988).

Frend, W.H.C., *The Early Church: From the Beginnings to 461* (Hodder & Stoughton, 1965).

Gill, R., *Churchgoing and Christian Ethics* (Cambridge: Cambridge University Press, 1999).

Greene, M., *Supporting Christians at Work* ('How to' Guide, 2.6), (Sheffield: Administry, 2001).

Greene, M., *Thank God It's Monday* (Milton Keynes: Scripture Union, 2001).

Gunton, C., *The Triune Creator* (Edinburgh: Edinburgh University Press, 1998).

Hallman, D.G., *Ecotheology: Voices from the South and North* (New York: Orbis, 1995).

Hardy, D.W., *God's Ways With the World: Thinking and Practising Christian Faith* (Edinburgh: T&T Clark, 1999).

Hardy, D.W. and D.F. Ford, *Jubilate: Theology in Praise* (London: Darton, Longman & Todd, 1984).

Hay, D., *Exploring Inner Space: Scientists and Religious Experience* (London: Mowbray,1987).

Hippolytus, *On the Apostolic Tradition*, tr. A. Stewart-Sykes (Crestwood, N.Y.: St. Vladimir's Seminary Press, 2001).

Hollenweger, W.J., *Pentecostalism, Origins and Developments Worldwide* (Peabody, Mass.: Hendrickson, 1997).

Hollenweger, W.J., *The Pentecostals* (London: SCM, 1972).

Kavanagh, A., *On Liturgical Theology* (Collegeville: Liturgical Press, 1984).

Kelsey, M.T., *Encounter with God: A Theology of Christian Experience* (Minneapolis: Bethany House, 1972).

Kleist, James A., *Ancient Christian Writers, vol. 6: The Didache, the Epistles of Barnabas, the Epistles and Martyrdom of St Polycarp, the Fragments of Papias* (Maryland: Newman Press and London: Longmans Green, 1948).

Kreider, A., *Worship and Evangelism in Pre-Christendom* (Joint Liturgical Studies, 32), (Cambridge: Grove Books, 1995).

Larive, A., *After Sunday: A Theology of Work* (New York and London: Continuum, 2004).

Lossky, V., *The Mystical Theology of the Eastern Church* (London: J. Clarke, 1957).

Lossky, V., *Orthodox Theology: An Introduction* (Crestwood: N.Y.: St. Vladimir's Seminary Press, 1989).

Luther, M., 'Liturgy and Hymn', *Luther's Works*, ed. U. Leupold, vols 36, 53 (Philadelphia: Fortress Press, 1965).

MacKinnon, M.H. and M. McIntyre, *Readings in Ecology and Feminist Theology* (Kansas: Sheed & Ward, 1995).

Macquarrie, J., *Paths in Spirituality* (London: SCM, 1972)

McFague, S., *Body of God: An Ecological Theology* (London: SCM,1993).

McFague, S., *Speaking in Parables: A Study in Metaphor and Theology* (London: SCM, 1975).

McGrath, A.E., *Christian Theology: An Introduction* (Oxford: Blackwell, 20013).

Mead, L.B., *The Once and Future Church: Reinventing the Congregation for a New Mission Frontier* (Washington: The Alban Institute, 1991).

Meek, D., *The Quest for Celtic Christianity* (Edinburgh: Handsel, 2000).

Meyendorff, J., *Byzantine Theology: Historical Trends and Doctrinal Themes* (New York: Fordham University Press, 1979).

Millward, C., *Renewing Harvest: Celebrating God's Creation* (Edinburgh, Cambridge and Durham: Pentland Press, 2001).

Minns, D., *Irenaeus* (London: Geoffrey Chapman, 1994).

Mitton, M., *Restoring the Woven Cord: Principles of Celtic Christianity for the Church Today* (London: Darton, Longman & Todd, 1995).

Moltmann, J., *The Church in the Power of the Spirit: A Contribution to Messianic Ecclesiology* (London: SCM, 1992²).

Moltmann, J., *God in Creation: An Ecological Doctrine of Creation* (London: SCM, 1985).

Morgenthaler, S., *Worship Evangelism: Inviting Unbelievers into the Presence of God* (Grand Rapids: Zondervan, 1995).

Mudge, L.S. (ed.), *Paul Ricoeur: Essays on Biblical Interpretation* (London: SPCK, 1981).

Niebuhr, R., *Christ and Culture* (New York and London: Harper & Row, 1951).

Old, H.O., *Worship: Reformed According to Scripture* (Louisville: Westminster John Knox, 2002).

Page, N., *And Now Let's Move into a Time of Nonsense: Why Worship Songs are Failing the Church* (Milton Keynes: Authentic Media, 2004).

Parry, R., *Worshipping Trinity: Coming Back to the Heart of Worship* (Carlisle: Paternoster, 2005).

Payne, E., *Baptist Principles* (London: Carey Kingsgate Press, 1944).

Paul VI, Pope, *Dei Verbum* (Dogmatic Constitution on Divine Revelation, 18 November 1965).

Paul VI, Pope, *Evangelii Nuntiandi: Evangelization in the Modern World* (Encyclical of Pope Paul VI, 8 December 1975).

Paul VI, Pope, *Gaudium et Spes* (Pastoral Constitution (1) On the Church in the Modern World, 7 December 1965).

Paul VI, Pope, *Sacrosanctum Concilium* (Second Vatican Council, Constitution on the Sacred Liturgy, 14 December 1963).

Peterson, D., *Engaging with God: A Biblical Theology of Worship* (Leicester: InterVarsity Press, 1992).

Pius X, Pope, *Inter Sollicitudines* (Motu Proprio of Pope St Pius X on Sacred Music, 22 November 1903), <www.unavoce.org/intersollicitudines.htm>.

Ramshaw, E. and D. S. Browning, *Ritual and Pastoral Care* (Philadelphia: Fortress Press, 1987).

Richter, P.J. and L.J. Francis, *Gone But Not Forgotten: Church Leaving and Returning* (London: Darton, Longman & Todd, 1998).

Ricoeur, P., *Interpretation Theory: Discourse and the Surplus of Meaning* (Fort Worth: Texas Christian University Press, 1976).

Ricoeur, P., *The Rule of Metaphor: The Creation of Meaning in Language* (London: Routledge & Keegan Paul, 1978).

Ridderbos, H., *Paul: An Outline of His Theology* (London: SPCK, 1977).

Roberts, A. and J. Donaldson (eds) *The Ante-Nicene Fathers: The Writings of the Fathers down to AD 325, vol. 1, The Apostolic Fathers with Justin Martyr and Irenaeus* (American reprint of the Edinburgh edition, Cleveland Coxe (ed.) (Edinburgh: T&T Clark and Grand Rapids: Eerdmans, 1989)).

Roman Catholic Church, *Catechism of the Catholic Church* (London: G. Chapman, 1994).

Routley, E., *Hymns Today and Tomorrow* (Nashville: Abingdon Press, 1964).

Rowe, D.J., *Faith at Work: A Celebration of All We Do* (Macon: Smith & Helwys, 1994).

Ryken, L., J. Wilhoit, T. Longman, C. Duriez, D. Penney and D.G. Reid (eds), *Dictionary of Biblical Imagery: An Encyclopaedic Exploration of the Images, Symbols, Motifs, Metaphors, Figures of Speech and Literary Patterns of the Bible* (Leicester: InterVarsity Press, 1998).

Santmire, H.P., *Ritualizing Nature: Renewing Christian Liturgy in a Time of Crisis* (Minneapolis: Fortress Press, 2008).

Schaff, P. and H. Wace (eds), *A Select Library of the Nicene and Post-Nicene Fathers of the Christian Church, Second Series, vol. 1* (Grand Rapids: Eerdmans, 1989).

Schmemann, A., *For the Life of the World: Sacraments and Orthodoxy* (Crestwood, N.Y.: St. Vladimir's Seminary Press, 1973).

Schmemann, A., *Introduction to Liturgical Theology* (Portland Maine: American Orthodox Press and Leighton Buzzard: Faith Press, 1966).

Simkins, R., *Creator and Creation: Nature in the Worldview of Ancient Israel* (Peabody, Mass.: Hendrickson, 1994).

Simpson, R., *Exploring Celtic Spirituality* (London: Hodder & Stoughton, 1995).

Smail, T., A. Walker and N. Wright, *Charismatic Renewal: The Search for a Theology* (London: SPCK, 1993).

Spinks, B., *The Sanctus in the Eucharistic Prayer* (Cambridge: Cambridge University Press, 1991).

Spinks, B. and I. Torrance (eds), *To Glorify God: Essays on Modern Reformed Liturgy* (Edinburgh: T&T Clark, 1999).

Stamoolis, J., *Eastern Orthodox Mission Theology Today* (New York: Orbis, 1986).

Staniloae, D., *Orthodox Dogmatic Theology: The Experience of God, vol. 1: Revelation and Knowledge of the Triune God* (Brookline, Mass.: Holy Cross Orthodox Press, 1994).

Steven, J.H.S., *Worship in the Spirit: Charismatic Worship in the Church of England* (Carlisle: Paternoster, 2002).

Stevenson, J. (ed.), *Creeds, Councils and Controversies: Documents Illustrating the History of the Church A.D. 337–461* (London: SPCK, 1972).

Thiselton, A., *Language, Liturgy and Meaning* (Nottingham: Grove Books, 1975).

Thiselton, A., *New Horizons in Hermeneutics: The Theory and Practice of Transforming Bible Reading* (London: Collins, 1992).

Thompson, J., *Christ in Perspective in the Theology of Karl Barth* (Edinburgh: Saint Andrew Press, 1978).

Torrance, J., *Worship, Community and the Triune God of Grace* (Carlisle: Paternoster, 1996).

Underhill, E., *Worship* (London: Nisbet, 1936).

Volf, M., *Work in the Spirit: Toward a Theology of Work* (Oxford: OUP, 1991).

Wainwright, G., *Doxology: The Praise of God in Worship, Doctrine and Life* (London: Epworth Press, 1980).

Walsh, M.J., *Commentary on the Catechism of the Catholic Church* (London: Geoffrey Chapman, 1994).

Ware, K., *The Inner Kingdom: Volume 1 of the Collected Works* (Crestwood, N.Y.: St. Vladimir's Seminary Press, 2001).

Webber, R., *Ancient-future Faith: Rethinking Evangelicalism for a Postmodern World* (Grand Rapids, Mich.: Baker, 1999).

Westermann, C., *Creation* (London: SPCK, 1974).

Westermann, C., *Der Segen in der Bibel und im Handeln der Kirche* (München: Kaiser, 1968), *Blessing in the Bible and the Life of the Church*, tr. K. Crim (Philadelphia: Fortress, 1978).

Westermann, C., *Elements of Old Testament Theology*, tr. D.W. Scott (Atlanta: John Knox, 1982).

White, J., *A Brief History of Christian Worship* (Nashville: Abingdon, 1993).

White, J., *Introduction to Christian Worship* (Nashville: Abingdon, 1980).

White, J., *Protestant Worship: Traditions in Transition* (Louisville: Westminster John Knox, 1989).

Whybrew, H., *The Orthodox Liturgy: Development of the Eucharistic Liturgy in the Byzantine Rite* (London: SPCK, 1989).

Wimber, J. and K. Springer, *Power Evangelism* (London: Hodder & Stoughton, 1985).

Witvliet, J., *Worship Seeking Understanding: Windows into Christian Practice* (Grand Rapids: Baker Academic, 2003).

Wright, N.T., *New Heavens, New Earth: The Biblical Picture of Christian Hope* (Cambridge: Grove Books, 1999).

Yong, A., *Beyond the Impasse: Toward a Pneumatological Theology of Religions* (Grand Rapids: Baker Academic, 2003).

Articles, publications and journals

Atherton, J., 'Trust Building Today: Tasks for Public Faith and Church', *The Bible in Transmission* (Autumn 2004), 9–11

Australian Bureau of Statistics, *Environmental Issues: People's Views and Practices* (Canberra, 1996).

Barrett, D., 'Annual Statistical Tables on Global Mission – 1997', *The International Bulletin of Missionary Research*, 21.1 (1997).

Black, A. 'Does Religion Impact on Environmentally Related Behaviour?', *Australian Association of Religion Review*, 9.2 (1996), 40–7.

Bria, I., 'Dynamics of Liturgy in Mission' *International Review of Mission*, 82.327 (1993).

Bria, I., 'Dynamics of Liturgy in Mission' (Report on the seminar 'Renewal of Orthodox worship' of the WCC sub-unit on Renewal and Congregational Life, Bucharest, October 1991), *International Review of Mission*, 82.327 (1993), 317–25.

Daneel, M.L., 'African Independent Church Pneumatology and the Salvation of all Creation', *International Review of Mission*, 82.326 (1993), 143–66.

Earey, M., 'This is the Word of the Lord: The Bible and Worship', *Anvil*, 19.2 (2002).

Elliott, E., J. Regens and B. Seldon, 'Exploring Variations in Public Support for Environmental Protection', *Social Science Quarterly*, 76.1 (1995), 41–52.

Ephrem the Syrian, 'A Hymn Against Bar-Daisan', tr. A.S. Duncan Jones, *Journal of Theological Studies*, vol. 5 (1904), 546ff.

Evans, M., J. Kelley, C. Bean and K. Zagorsky, *The National Social Science Survey*, data file (Research School of Social Sciences, Australian National University, 1994).

Fach, S., *Ascended Christ: Mediator of our Worship*, unpublished paper for Spurgeon's College Post-graduate Seminar, 8 January 2004.

Ford, D., 'Coping with being overwhelmed', *The Bible in Transmission* (Swindon: Bible Society, Autumn 1997), 8–10.

Greeley, A., 'Religion and Attitudes Towards the Environment', *The Journal for the Scientific Study of Religion*, 32.1 (1993), 19–28.

Hughes, P., *Values and Religion: A Case Study of Environmental Concern and Christian Beliefs and Practices among Australians*, *Christian Research Association* research paper no. 3 (1997).

Marshall, I.H., 'How far did the early Christians worship God?', *Churchman*, 99 (1985), 216–99.

Methodist Church, *Marriage in the Methodist Church*, report for the Wolverhampton Methodist Conference, July 2002.

Phillips, D., 'Trends in Common Worship', *Churchman*, 112.2 (1998), 102–16.

Sheldrake, P., 'Celtic Spirituality', *Evangel*, 15.3 (1997), 74–6.

Sochaczewski, P., 'Zimbabwe's "war of the trees" fights on holy ground' *Gemini News Service* (May 1996), <www.Sochaczewski.com/ARTtzirrcon.html>.

Steven, J., 'Charismatic Hymnody in the Light of Early Methodist Hymnody', *Studia Liturgica*, 26.2 (1997), 217–34.

Streeter, S., 'A New Testament Perspective on Worship', *Evangelical Quarterly*, 68.3 (1996), 209–21.

Triebel, J., 'Living Together with the Ancestors: Ancestor Veneration in Africa as a Challenge for Missiology', *Missiology, An International Review*, 30.2 (2002), 187–97.

Trivasse, K., 'My pinching shoes', *Contact: The Interdisciplinary Journal of Pastoral Studies*, 137 (2002), 25–31.

White, L., 'The Historical Roots of our Ecological Crisis', *Science*, 155 (1967), 1203–07, reprinted in MacKinnon, M. and M. McIntyre, *Readings in Ecology and Feminist Theology* (Kansas: Sheed & Ward, 1995), 25–35.

Endnotes

1. Setting the Scene

[1] Charles H. Spurgeon, *Spurgeon's Prayers* (Fearn, Ross-shire: Christian Focus, 1993), 146.

[2] For transcripts of services from 2000–2003, see Chris Voke, *Christian Corporate Worship and the Doctrine of Creation*, doctoral dissertation (University of Wales, 2005).

[3] The Roman Catholic Church, *The Sunday Missal* (London: CollinsLiturgical, 1984).

[4] The Greek Orthodox Church, *The Divine Liturgy of our father among the saints, John Chrysostom: The Greek text together with a translation into English* (Oxford: Oxford University Press, 1995).

[5] Herman N. Ridderbos, *Paul: An Outline of His Theology* (London: SPCK, 1977), 486; Howard I. Marshall, 'How far did the early Christians worship God?', *Churchman*, 99 (1985), 216–99; David Peterson, *Engaging with God: A Biblical Theology of Worship* (Leicester: InterVarsity Press, 1992), 150, 219.

[6] Romans 12:1.

[7] 1 Peter 2:5,9,11–12.

2. Knowing, Believing and Ecology

[1] Paul Ricoeur, 'Toward a Hermenuetic of the Idea of Revelation', *Harvard Theological Review*, 70.1–2 (January–April, 1997) in Lewis S. Mudge (ed.), *Paul Ricoeur: Essays on Biblical Interpretation* (London: SPCK, 1981), 73–118.

[2] Ricoeur in Mudge, *Essays*, 89f.

3 Trevor Hart, 'The Glory of Imagination and the Imagination of Glory' in John Colwell (ed.), *Called to One Hope: Perspectives on the Life to Come* (Carlisle: Paternoster, 2001), 229.

4 Hart in Colwell, *Called*, 237.

5 Psalm 73:17,28.

6 John Calvin, *Institutes of the Christian Religion*, tr. Henry Beveridge (London: James Clarke, 1957), II. 9, 2.

7 Vladimir Lossky, *Orthodox Theology: An Introduction* (Crestwood, N.Y.: St. Vladimir's Seminary Press, 1989), 21.

8 Donald Fairbairn, *Eastern Orthodoxy through Western Eyes* (Louisville and London: Westminster John Knox, 2002), 54–9.

9 Evagrios of Pontus, *The Praktikos: Chapters on Prayer*, tr. John E. Bamberger (Spencer, Mass.: Cistercian Publications, 1970), 65.

10 John D. Witvliet, *Worship Seeking Understanding: Windows into Christian Practice* (Grand Rapids: Baker Academic, 2003), 17; Christopher J. Ellis, *Gathering: A Theology and Spirituality of Worship in Free Church Tradition* (London: SCM, 2004), 2. See also Robin Parry, *Worshipping Trinity: Coming Back to the Heart of Worship* (Carlisle: Paternoster, 2005); John E. Colwell, *The Rhythm of Doctrine: A Liturgical Sketch of Christian Faith and Faithfulness* (Milton Keynes: Paternoster, 2007).

11 Alister McGrath, *Christian Theology: An Introduction* (Oxford: Blackwell, 20013), 189.

12 Martin Luther, 'Liturgy and Hymns', *Luther's Works*, vol. 53, ed. Ulrich Leupold (Philadelphia: Fortress Press, 1965), xiii.

13 Walter J. Hollenweger, *The Pentecostals* (London: SCM, 1972), 160.

14 Hollenweger, *Pentecostals*, 464.

15 Witvliet, *Worship Seeking*, 17.

16 Erik Routley in his Preface to *Hymns Today and Tomorrow* (Nashville: Abingdon Press, 1964).

17 Jeff Astley and David Day (eds), *The Contours of Christian Education* (Great Wakering: McCrimmons, 1992), 141–52.

18 John H. Westerhoff (ed.), *A Colloquy on Christian Education* (Philadelphia: Pilgrim Press, 1972), 64f.

19 Karl Barth, *Church Dogmatics* (Edinburgh: T&T Clark, 1975), IV/2, 112–13.

20 John G. Davies (ed.) in the Preface to *A New Dictionary of Liturgy and Worship* (London: SCM, 1986).

21 Davies, *New Dictionary*, 506.

22 Aidan Kavanagh, *On Liturgical Theology* (Collegeville: Liturgical Press, 1984), 74f.

23 John Calvin, 'The Necessity of Reforming the Church' in *Tracts Relating to the Reformation*, tr. H. Beveridge (Edinburgh: Calvin Translation Society, 1844), 126.

24 D.A. Carson, *Worship by the Book* (Grand Rapids, Mich.: Zondervan, 2002), 16f.

25 Davies, *New Dictionary*, 506.

26 James Torrance, *Worship, Community and the Triune God of Grace* (Carlisle: Paternoster, 1996), ix.

27 Lossky, *Orthodox Theology*, 57.

28 Walter Brueggemann, *Theology of the Old Testament* (Minneapolis: Fortress Press, 1997), 134.

29 Brueggemann, *Theology*, 126–30.

30 Brueggemann, *Theology*, 107.

31 R. Berry, *God's Book of Works* (London: T&T Clark, 2003), 131.

32 Lynn White, 'The Historical Roots of our Ecological Crisis', *Science*, 155 (1967), 1203–7, reprinted in Mary H. MacKinnon and Marie McIntyre, *Readings in Ecology and Feminist Theology* (Kansas: Sheed & Ward, 1995), 25–35.

33 Berry, *God's Book*, 83–6.

34 See the articles in R. Berry (ed.), *The Care of Creation: Focusing Concern and Action* (Leicester: InterVarsity Press, 2000).

35 Harvey Cox, *The Secular City* (London: SCM, 1965), 23.

36 Philip J. Hughes, *Values and Religion: A Case Study of Environmental Concern and Christian Beliefs and Practices among Australians*, Christian Research Association, research paper no. 3 (1997).

37 John Black, *The Dominion of Man: The Search for Ecological Responsibility* (Edinburgh: Edinburgh University Press, 1970), 29–43.

38 White, 'The Historical Roots', 26.

39 Jürgen Moltmann, *God in Creation: An Ecological Doctrine of Creation* (London: SCM, 1985), 13.

40 Geoffrey Wainwright, *Doxology: The Praise of God in Worship, Doctrine and Life* (London: Epworth Press, 1980), 119.

41 Loren B. Mead, *The Once and Future Church: Reinventing the Congregation for a New Mission Frontier* (Washington: The Alban Institute, 1991), 27, 43.

42 Wainwright, *Doxology*, 120.

[43] Using H. Richard Niebuhr's analysis of Christianity and culture from *Christ and Culture* (New York and London: Harper & Row, 1951), and the exploration of contextual theological method in Stephen B. Bevans, *Models of Contextual Theology* (New York: Orbis, 1992).

[44] Witvliet, *Worship Seeking*, 115.

[45] Witvliet, *Worship Seeking*, 116.

3. Worship, Behavior and Mission

[1] Berry, *God's Book*, xii.

[2] World Conservation Strategy, *Caring for the Earth* (1980, revised), (Gland, Switzerland: IUNC, WWF, UNEP, 1991).

[3] J. Atherton, 'Trust Building Today: Tasks for Public Faith and Church', *The Bible in Transmission* (Autumn, 2004), 10.

[4] K. Trivasse, 'My pinching shoes', *Contact: The Interdisciplinary Journal of Pastoral Studies*, 137 (2002), 31.

[5] Ernest Payne, *Baptist Principles* (London: Carey Kingsgate Press, 1944), 90.

[6] Robin Gill, *Churchgoing and Christian Ethics* (Cambridge: Cambridge University Press, 1999), 197–9.

[7] Philip J. Richter and Leslie J. Francis, *Gone But Not Forgotten: Church Leaving and Returning* (London: Darton, Longman & Todd, 1998), 119.

[8] Richter and Francis, *Gone*, 147.

[9] Richter and Francis, *Gone*, 151.

[10] G. Preece, 'The Threefold Call: The Trinitarian Character of Our Everyday Vocations' in Robert J. Banks, *Faith Goes to Work: Reflections from the Marketplace* (New York: Alban Institute, 1993), 164.

[11] Paul Chung, *Spirituality and Social Ethics in John Calvin: A Pneumatological Perspective* (Lanham: University Press of America, 2000), 18.

[12] Jürgen Moltmann, *The Church in the Power of the Spirit: A Contribution to Messianic Ecclesiology* (London: SCM, 19922); and *God in Creation* (1985).

[13] Jürgen Moltmann, *The Spirit of Life: A Universal Affirmation* (London: SCM, 1992), x. See also Miroslav Volf, *Work in the Spirit: Towards a Theology of Work* (Oxford: Oxford University Press, 1991).

[14] Dr Bill Allen, *Tutor in Pastoral Studies*, Spurgeon's College, 1992–9.

[15] Robert Banks, *Faith Goes to Work: Reflections from the Marketplace* (New York: Alban Institute, 1993).

[16] David J. Rowe, *Faith at Work: A Celebration of All We Do* (Macon: Smith & Helwys, 1994), 107–9.

[17] Mark Greene, *Supporting Christians at Work* ('How to' Guide, 2.6), (Sheffield: Administry, 2001); Mark Greene, *Thank God It's Monday* (London: Scripture Union, 2001).

[18] A. Messer (ed.) in the header of *Workwise*, London Institute of Contemporary Christianity, 2003 onwards, 2; and see <www.licc.org.uk/work/>.

[19] Armand Larive, *After Sunday: A Theology of Work* (New York and London: Continuum, 2004), 89, 164f.

[20] H. Paul Santmire, *Ritualizing Nature: Renewing Christian Liturgy in a Time of Crisis* (Minneapolis: Fortress Press, 2008), 51.

[21] David Ford, 'Coping with being overwhelmed', *The Bible in Transmission* (Swindon: Bible Society, Autumn 1997), 8.

[22] Ford, 'Coping', 8.

[23] *How Green is Your Church?* (Nottingham City Council and Soundworks, 1993).

[24] < www.earthministry.org>.

[25] M. Evans, J. Kelley, C. Bean and K. Zagorsky, *The National Social Science Survey*, data file (Research School of Social Sciences, Australian National University, 1994); *Environmental Issues: People's Views and Practices* (Canberra: Australian Bureau of Statistics, 1996).

[26] Hughes, *Values and Religion*, 2.

[27] G. Halford, 'Human Decision-making about Environmental Change' in H. Brookfield and L. Doube, *Global Change: The Human Dimension* (Canberra: Academy of the Social Sciences, Australian National University, 1990), 38.

[28] E. Elliott, J. Regens and B. Seldon, 'Exploring Variations in Public Support for Environmental Protection', *Social Science Quarterly*, 76.1 (1995), 41–52.

[29] Evans et al, *Environmental Issues*.

[30] A. Black, 'Does Religion Impact on Environmentally Related Behaviour?', *Australian Association of Religion Review*, 9.2 (1996), 40–7.

[31] Hughes, *Values and Religion*, 14, 17. This is also the conclusion of Andrew Greeley in 'Religion and Attitudes Towards the Environment', *The Journal for the Scientific Study of Religion*, 32.1 (1993), 19–28.

[32] D. Sherkat, and C. Ellison, 'Structuring the Religion–Environment Connection: Identifying Religious Influences on Environmental Concern and Activism', *Journal for the Scientific Study of Religion*, 46.1 (March 2007), 71–85.

[33] Hughes, *Values and Religion*, 20.

[34] Hughes, *Values and Religion*, 23.

[35] Santmire, *Ritualizing*, 91.

[36] Acts 5:13.

[37] 1 Corinthians 14:23–25.

[38] Justin, Apology, I, 61–7; James Stevenson and W.H.C.Frend (eds), *A New Eusebius: Documents Illustrating the History of the Church to AD 337* (London: SPCK, rev. ed. 1972), 63f.

[39] Stevenson and Frend, *New Eusebius*, 62.

[40] Pope Paul VI, *Evangelii Nuntiandi: Evangelization in the Modern World* (Encyclical of Pope Paul VI, 8 December 1975), sect. 43.

[41] Pope John Paul II, *Redemptoris Missio* (Encyclical of John Paul II on the permanent validity of the Church's missionary mandate, 7 December 1990). 21.

[42] *Redemptoris Missio*, 31.

[43] I. Bria, 'Dynamics of Liturgy in Mission' (Report on the seminar 'Renewal of Orthodox worship' of the WCC sub-unit on Renewal and Congregational Life, Bucharest, October 1991), *International Review of Mission*, 82.327 (1993), 317.

[44] James Stamoolis, *Eastern Orthodox Mission Theology Today* (New York: Orbis, 1986), 50–55.

[45] *In Tune with Heaven: The Report of the Archbishop's Commission on Church Music* (London: Church House Publishing, 1992), 17.

[46] *In Tune with Heaven*, 37.

[47] Graham Kendrick (ed.), *Ten Worshipping Churches* (London: MARC Europe, 1987), 18.

[48] Peter Craig-Wild, *Tools for Transformation: Making Worship Work* (London: Darton, Longman & Todd, 2002), 23.

[49] Witvliet, *Worship Seeking*, 92.

[50] Sally Morgenthaler, *Worship Evangelism: Inviting Unbelievers to the Presence of God* (Grand Rapids: Zondervan, 1995), 102.

[51] Romans 1:20.

[52] John Finney, *Finding Faith Today: How Does it Happen?* (Swindon: The Bible Society, 1992).

[53] E. Bailey, *Implicit Religion: An Introduction* (London: Middlesex University Press, 1998), 21, 26.

[54] G. Barna, *The Barna Report: What Americans Believe* (Ventura, Calif.: Regal, 1991), 169; Morton T. Kelsey, *Encounter with God: A Theology of Christian Experience* (Minneapolis: Bethany House, 1972), 151.

[55] David Hay, *Exploring Inner Space: Scientists and Religious Experience* (London: Mowbray, 1987).

[56] F. Senn, '"Worship Alive": An analysis and critique of "Alternative Worship Services"', *Worship*, 69.3 (1995), 194–234.

[57] Brian Draper and Kevin Draper, *Refreshing Worship* (Oxford: The Bible Reading Fellowship, 2000), 18

[58] Schmemann, *Liturgical Theology*, 96.

[59] Schmemann, *Liturgical Theology*, 112.

[60] *Marriage in the Methodist Church*, report for the Wolverhampton Methodist Conference, July 2002, reported in the *Baptist Times*, 13 June 2002.

[61] Morgenthaler, *Worship Evangelism*, 216.

[62] Morgenthaler, *Worship Evangelism*, 233.

4. The Christian Doctrine of Creation

[1] The set liturgies fall into two groups. The first group comprises older material, generally available in the denominational service books up to the late 1980s, with the exception of the Orthodox liturgy, which is a new translation of the ancient Greek text. The first group is:

> *A Manual for Ministers* (the Congregational Union, 1936)
>
> *The Alternative Service Book* (the Church of England, 1980)
>
> *The Book of Common Prayer* (the Church of England, 1662/1892)
>
> *The Divine Liturgy of our father among the saints John Chrysostom* (the Greek Orthodox, ET, 1995)
>
> *The Missal in Latin and English* (the Roman Catholic Church, 1952)
>
> *The Sunday Missal* (the Roman Catholic Church, 1984)
>
> *The United Reformed Church Service Book* (the United Reformed Church, 1989)
>
> *Orders and Prayers for Church Worship* (the Baptist Union, 1960).

The second group, more recent, often with radically altered liturgical material, consists of:

> *Book of Common Order of the Church of Scotland* (Church of Scotland, 1996)
>
> *Book of Common Worship* (the Presbyterian Church of the USA, 1993)
>
> *Common Worship: Services and Prayers for the Church of England* (the Church of England, 2000)

Gathering for Worship: Patterns and Prayers for the Community of Disciples (Christopher J. Ellis and Myra Blyth (eds) for the Baptist Union of Great Britain, 2005)

Patterns and Prayers for Christian Worship (the Baptist Union, 1991)

The Methodist Worship Book (the Methodist Church, 1999)

Worship for the United Reformed Church (the United Reformed Church, 2003)

[2] Transcripts of services 2000–2003 in Voke, *Christian Corporate Worship*.

[3] Genesis 1:1.

[4] Hebrews 1:10; John 1:1, etc.

[5] 2 Maccabees 7:28; 2 Baruch 21:4; 2 Enoch 25:1ff.

[6] Hebrews 11:3

[7] John 1:3; Acts 17:24; Revelation 4:11, etc.

[8] F.F. Bruce, *The Epistle to the Hebrews* (London: Marshall, Morgan & Scott, 1964), 281, note 23.

[9] Genesis 1:14ff.

[10] *Miss.*, 697 and 717.

[11] *SMiss.*, 34.

[12] The Baptist Union, *PP*, 32

[13] The Methodist Church, *MWB*, 31

[14] The Greek Orthodox Church, *DL*, 40.

[15] Pss. 2:4; 8:1.

[16] Pss. 93; 47; 96:13; 145:9.

[17] Irenaeus, *Adversus Haereses*, chap. III, *ANF*, 418f.

[18] Denis Minns, *Irenaeus* (London: Geoffrey Chapman, 1994), 34.

[19] Paul Brockelman, *Cosmology and Creation: The Spiritual Significance of Contemporary Cosmology* (Oxford: Oxford University Press, 1999), 34, 36.

[20] Charles Hartshorne, *Man's Vision of God and the Logic of Theism* (Chicago and New York: Willett, Clark & Co., 1941 and 1962).

[21] Sallie McFague, *Body of God: An Ecological Theology* (London: SCM, 1993), 20f.

[22] McFague, *Body of God*, 153ff.

[23] See Santmire, *Ritualizing*, 109.

[24] Evelyn Underhill, *Worship* (London: Nisbet, 1936), 262f.

[25] *DL*, 6f.

[26] *DL*, 31.

[27] *DL*, 40.

[28] McGrath, *Christian Theology*, 297.

[29] Genesis 1:29–30.

[30] Deuteronomy 11:14–15.

[31] 1 Timothy 4:3–4.

[32] 2 Corinthians 9:8–10.

[33] Colin E. Gunton, *The Triune Creator* (Edinburgh: Edinburgh University Press, 1998), 10.

[34] James A. Kleist, *Ancient Christian Writers*, vol. 6, *The Didache, The Epistles of Barnabas, The Epistles and Martyrdom of St Polycarp, The Fragments of Papias* (Maryland: Newman Press and London: Longmans Green, 1948), 21.

[35] Clement, *The First Epistle of Clement*, Chapter XXXIV, ANF, 15.

[36] Exodus 31:3–5.

[37] Psalms 139:7.

[38] Acts 17:28; F.F. Bruce, *The Book of Acts* (London: Marshall Morgan & Scott, 1954), 359f.

[39] Irenaeus, *Adversus Haereses*, chap. IV, Preface, 4, and chap. V, 6.1, ANF, 463, 531.

[40] Irenaeus, *Adversus Haereses*, chap. IV, 20.1, 487f.

[41] Irenaeus, *Adversus Haereses*, 31.2, 33.1, 505f.

[42] Gunton, *The Triune Creator*, 8f.

[43] Bryan D. Spinks, *The Sanctus in the Eucharistic Prayer* (Cambridge: Cambridge University Press, 1991).

[44] Ephrem the Syrian, 'A Hymn Against Bar-Daisan', tr. A.S. Duncan Jones, *Journal of Theological Studies*, 5 (1904), 546ff.

[45] John 1:3; Col. 1:16–17; Heb. 1:2,10.

[46] Psalms 102:25.

[47] Tertullian, *Against Hermogenes*, 45, ANF, 502.

[48] Irenaeus, *Adversus Haereses*, chap. V, 18.3, 546.

[49] *DL*, 1995, 22f.

[50] *Cat.* paras 456–60; J. Dupuis, 'The Incarnation of the Son' in M. Walsh, *Commentary on the Catechism of the Catholic Church* (London: Chapman, 1994), 118.

[51] Calvin, *Inst.*, 2.12.4, 402f.

[52] John 6:51.

[53] *DL*, 8.

[54] *DL*, 143

[55] Gunton, *Triune Creator*, 124.

[56] Genesis 1:31.

[57] *OP*, 72f.

[58] *MM*, 21, 22, 25, 33.

59 Sinclair B. Ferguson and David Wright (eds), *New Dictionary of Theology* (Leicester: InterVarsity Press, 1988), 454.

60 MM, 34, 37, 38.

61 Miss., 749.

62 J. Mays, '"Maker of Heaven and Earth": Creation in the Psalms', in William P. Brown and Susan D. McBride Jr. (eds), *God Who Creates: Essays in Honor of W. Sibley Towner* (Grand Rapids: Eerdmans, 2000), 77f.

63 Quoted in McFague, *Body of God*, 167, note 30.

64 Hallman, *Ecotheology*, 5; and see White, 'The Historical Roots', 25–35.

65 McFague, *Body of God*, 167.

66 McFague, *Body of God*, 67f., 91f.

67 Ronald Simkins, *Creator and Creation: Nature in the Worldview of Ancient Israel* (Peabody, Mass.: Hendrickson, 1994), 33–9.

68 Gunton, *Triune Creator*, 12.

69 J. Bagertscher, *The Religion of Nature and the Nature of Religion*, unpublished paper to the Network for the Study of Implicit Religion, Denton Conference, 1999, 13.

70 W. Storrar, 'From Brave Heart to Faint Heart: Worship and culture in post-modern Scotland' in Bryan Spinks and Iain Torrance (eds), *To Glorify God: Essays on Modern Reformed Liturgy* (Edinburgh: T&T Clark, 1999), 75.

71 J. Wootton, *Introducing a Practical Feminist Theology of Worship* (Sheffield: Sheffield Academic Press, 2000), 119.

72 J. Cunanan, 'The Prophet of Environment and Development' in Hallman, *Ecotheology*, 15ff.

73 Joel 1:13–20; 2:14–17.

74 Joel 2:14,19; 3:18.

75 Romans 8:22f.

76 Gunton, *Triune Creator*, 11.

77 Gunton, *Triune Creator*, 12.

78 Basil the Great, *The Book of Saint Basil on the Spirit* (Crestwood, N.Y.: St. Vladimir's Seminary Press, 1988), sections IX and XVI, 43, 66.

79 1 Corinthians 11:26.

80 Irenaeus, *Adversus Haereses*, chap. V, 13.1, 562.

81 N.T. Wright, 'New Heavens, New Earth' in Colwell, *Called*, 32.

82 Wright, 'New Heavens' 47.

83 *Miss.*, 741ff.

5. Contemporary Efforts – Problems and Possibilities

[1] The present revival of interest in things Celtic is wider than the church. Attention to the history, languages and traditions of Celtic roots within the British Isles is apparent throughout today's society. In the church this influence has been primarily through the collection and creation of material for private prayer and public worship. Christian interest in Celtic liturgy began with the 1960's rediscovery of Alexander Carmichael's *Carmina Gadelica* (A. Carmichael and J. MacInnes [ed.], *Charms of the Gaels: Hymns and Incantations* [Edinburgh: Floris Books, 1992]), a nineteenth-century collection of both older and more recent Scottish hymns, prayers and poems. Celtic worship is therefore, in fact, a set of theological emphases and liturgical practices not directly related to the Celtic church of the fifth to twelfth centuries, or to any of its revivals over the last thousand years, but freshly stimulated in response to contemporary needs. Not least of these needs is a desire to incorporate creation spirituality into prayer and worship.

[2] Donald E. Meek, *The Quest for Celtic Christianity* (Edinburgh: Handsel Press, 2000), 7.

[3] Iona Community, *Iona Abbey Worship Book* (Glasgow: Wild Goose Publications, 2001); Andy Raine and John T. Skinner, *Celtic Daily Prayer: A Northumbrian Office* (London: Marshall Pickering, 1994); Ray Simpson, *Celtic Worship through the Year: Prayers, Readings and Creative Activities for Ordinary Days and Saints' Days* (London: Hodder & Stoughton, 1997); Patricia Anne Robson, *A Celtic Liturgy* (London: HarperCollins, 2000).

[4] The Church of Scotland Panel on Worship, *Book of Common Order of the Church of Scotland* (Edinburgh: St Andrew Press, 1960), 35–40, 145–55, 425, 553, 557, 596–8.

[5] Iona Community, *Worship Book*, 60, 73, 83.

[6] Ray Simpson, *Exploring Celtic Spirituality* (London: Hodder & Stoughton, 1995), 58.

[7] Raine and Skinner, *Celtic Daily Prayer*, 3.

[8] John Macquarrie, *Paths in Spirituality* (London: SCM, 1972), 123.

[9] Michael Mitton, *Restoring the Woven Cord: Principles of Celtic Christianity for the Church Today* (London: Darton, Longman & Todd, 1995), 59.

[10] Macquarrie, *Paths* (1972), 123.

[11] I. Bradley, *The Celtic Way* (London: Darton, Longman & Todd, 1993), 35, 37; P. Murray (ed.), *The Deer's Cry: A Treasury of Irish Religious Verse* (Dublin: Four Courts Press, 1986), 15.

[12] Bradley, *The Celtic Way*, 34, 35.

[13] Meek, *The Quest*, 22, 31f.

[14] From *Carmina Gadelica*, quoted by Bradley in *The Celtic Way*, 34.

[15] Robson, *A Celtic Liturgy*, 35, 38.

[16] David Adam, *A Celtic Daily Prayer Companion* (London: Marshall Pickering, 1997), 53.

[17] The North American Conference on Religion and Ecology, 5 Thomas Circle, N.W., Washington, D.C., 2005.

[18] <www.webofcreation.org/Worship/resources/htm>, *Sample Liturgies*, 1990 and 1992.

[19] This is true also, but to a lesser extent, of 'alternative worship' texts from the UK, as in Jonny Baker, Doug Gay with Jenny Brown, *Alternative Worship* (London: SPCK, 2003).

[20] *Sample Liturgies*, 'Psalm of the Cosmos'.

[21] *Sample Liturgies*, 'Blessing of Fields and Crops' and 'Prayer of Praise'.

[22] *Sample Liturgies*, 'A Prayer of Awareness'.

[23] *Sample Liturgies*, 'Litany for God's Guidance'.

[24] *Sample Liturgies*, 'A Call to Prayer'.

[25] Annie Dillard, *Pilgrim at Tinker Creek* (New York: HarperCollins, 1974).

[26] *Sample Liturgies*, 'A Litany of Gratitude'.

[27] *Sample Liturgies*, 'A Litany for Healing'.

[28] Psalms 103:3.

[29] Amos 9:13–15; Isaiah 65:17–21; Jeremiah 31:3–5,11–14.

[30] Author unknown, 'A Litany for Healing', *Interfaith Declarations and Worship Observance Resources* (The North American Conference on Religion and Ecology, 5 Thomas Circle, N.W., Washington, D.C. 2005), 1990.

[31] Chief Seattle's words to President Franklin Pierce in December 1854, quoted in K. Krum and H.L. Antolini *An Environmental Stations of the Cross*, see <www.earthminisry.org>.

[32] Author unknown, 'Litany for Growth', *Sample Liturgies*, 1990.

[33] *A New Zealand Prayer Book* (Auckland: Collins, 1989), 181; quoted in the *Staffordshire Seven, Seasonal Worship from the Countryside* (London: SPCK, 2003), 227.

[34] John 17:3.

[35] J. Robinson, *Celebration: The Grail Liturgy* (Tywyn, Gwynedd: Grail Retreat, 2000), 2.

[36] Simpson, *Exploring*, 74f.

[37] 'A Celtic Eucharist' quoted in Simpson, *Exploring*, 61.

[38] Matthew Fox, *Creation Spirituality: Liberating Gifts for the Peoples of the Earth* (San Francisco: Harper, 1991) in Krum, K. and H.L. Antolini, *An Environmental Stations of the Cross* (St Brendan the Navigator Episcopal Church, Stonington, Maine, April 4 1994), <www.earthministry.org>.

[39] Marthinus L. Daneel, *African Earthkeepers*, vols 1 and 2 (Pretoria: University of South Africa, 1998 and 1999).

[40] Marthinus L. Daneel, 'African Independent Church Pneumatology and the Salvation of all Creation' in *International Review of Mission*, 82.326 (1993), 162.

[41] Colossians 1:20.

[42] Marinda, in Daneel, *African Earthkeepers*, vol. 2, 77.

[43] Bishop Chimhangwa, Sermon at Tree-planting Eucharist, ZAC headquarters, Masvingo district, 15 March 1992 in Daneel, *African Earthkeepers*, vol. 2, 369.

[44] Marinda in Daneel, *African Earthkeepers*, vol. 2, 366.

[45] Daneel, *African Earthkeepers*, vol. 2, 87, 89.

[46] Moltmann, *God in Creation*, 227.

[47] Daneel, *African Earthkeepers*, vol. 2, 88.

[48] Daneel, *African Earthkeepers*, vol. 2, 89.

[49] Genesis 1:22,28.

[50] Donald Fairbairn, *Eastern Orthodoxy*, 44, 43f.

[51] Kallistos Ware, *The Inner Kingdom: vol. 1 of the Collected Works* (Crestwood, N.Y.: St. Vladimir's Seminary Press, 2001), 67.

[52] P. Evdokimov, 'La sacerdoce universel des laïcs dans la tradition orientale' in Elchinger L. (ed.), *l'Eglise en dialogue* (Paris, 1962), 39f. in Ware, *Inner Kingdom*, 68.

[53] *DL*, 49f.

[54] Hugh Whybrew, *The Orthodox Liturgy: Development of the Eucharistic Language in the Byzantine Rite* (London: SPCK, 1989), 20; John R.K. Fenwick, *The Eastern Orthodox Liturgy* (Nottingham: Grove Books, 1978), 15.

[55] Fenwick, *Eastern Orthodox*, 24

[56] John Meyendorff in Daniel B. Clendenin (ed.), *Eastern Orthodox Theology: A Western Perspective* (Grand Rapids: Baker Academic, 2003), 90.

57 John Meyendorff, *Byzantine Theology: Historical Trends and Doctrinal Themes* (New York: Fordham University Press, 1979), 170.

58 < www.anastasis.org.uk/megagiasm.htm>.

59 Basil, *On the Spirit*, XV, 35.

60 Ambrose, *On the Holy Spirit*, L.I.c. VII, 88, *ANF*, 105.

61 Ware, *Inner Kingdom*, 71.

62 Pope John Paul II and Patriarch Bartholomew, 'Common Declaration on Environmental Ethics', *L'Osservatore Romano*, Weekly Edition in English, 12 June 2002 (Baltimore: The Cathedral Foundation), 5.

63 Fairbairn, *Eastern Orthodoxy*, 134.

64 Lossky, *Orthodox Theology*, 68–71.

65 Genesis 2:7.

66 Isaac the Syrian in Lossky, *Orthodox Theology*, 69.

67 Genesis 1:22,28.

68 Schmemann, *Liturgical Theology*, 46.

69 Claus Westermann, *Elements of Old Testament Theology*, tr. D.W. Scott (Atlanta: John Knox, 1982), 112, 114.

70 The Catholic Church, 'General Introduction', *Book of Blessings, approved for use in the dioceses of the United States of America by the National Conference of Catholic Bishops and confirmed by the Apostolic See* (Collegeville: Liturgical Press, 1989), xxiv.

71 P. Bishop, 'Sacramentals' in Fink, *The New Dictionary of Sacramental Worship* (Collegeville, Minn.: Liturgical Press, 1990), 1114f.

72 Pope Paul VI, *Sacrosanctum Concilium* (Second Vatican Council, Constitution on the Sacred Liturgy, 14 December 1963).

73 *Cat.*, 373, para. 1670.

74 Genesis 1:22.

75 Mark 7:18ff.

76 1 Timothy 4:3–4.

6. Worship in the Humanity of Christ

1 Hugh Whybrew, *The Orthodox Liturgy: Development of the Eucharistic Liturgy in the Byzantine Rite* (London: SPCK, 1989), 4.

2 Lossky, *Orthodox Theology*, 70–1; H. Auxention in Archimandrite Chrysostomos, *Contemporary Eastern Orthodox Thought: The Traditional Voice* (Belmont: Büchervertriebstanstalt, 1982), 8.

3 *Miss.*, 733; *SMiss.*, 43.

4 Luther, 'The Babylonian Captivity of the Church', *LW*, vol. 36, 35–48; Vilmos Vajta, *Luther on Worship: An Interpretation* (Philadelphia: Muhlenberg, 1958), 15.

5 J.J. von Allmen, *Worship: Its Theology and Practice* (London: Lutterworth, 1965), 23f.

6 Torrance, *Worship*, 18ff.

7 Acts 14:15–17.

8 Acts 17:27–28.

9 Romans 1:19–20.

10 Augustine, *The Works of Saint Augustine*, Part I, vol. 5, *The Trinity*, eds J. Rotell and E. Hill (New York: New City Press, 1991), book IX, 270–85; McGrath, *Christian Theology*, 213; Thomas Aquinas, *Summa Theologica*, II.2.2–4; Calvin, *Inst.* I.3.1–2 and I.6.1; J. Edwards, 'Images of Divine Things', Works, ed. H. Stout, vol. 11 (Yale, 1993 and 1997), 51–129; Minkema K. (ed.) 'God's All Sufficiency for the Supply of our Wants', vol. 14, 474–83; and see James Barr, *Biblical Faith and Natural Theology: The Gifford Lectures for 1991* (Oxford: Oxford University Press, 1993).

11 Underhill, *Worship*, 93.

12 Wainwright in Davies, *A New Dictionary*, 505.

13 Hebrews 1:7.

14 Hebrews 1:4,6.

15 1 Peter 1:12.

16 Clement, *First Epistle*, Ch XX, *ANF*, 14.

17 Cyril, *Mystagogical Catechesis 1*, Lecture XXIII, 'On Sacred Liturgy and Communion', 6, *ANF*, 154.

18 John Meyendorff, *Byzantine Theology: Historical Trends and Doctrinal Themes* (New York: Fordham University Press, 1979), 136.

19 Carson, *Worship by the Book*, 26.

20 Matthew 11:25–27; Luke 10:21–22.

21 Mark 14:26; John 17:9.

22 John 14:31.

23 Hughes Old, *Worship: Reformed According to Scripture* (Louisville: Westminster John Knox, 2002), 1.

24 Barth, *CD*, III/4, 36f.

25 Barth, *CD* I/2, 280–361.

26 Torrance, *Worship*, 10–11.

27 *Cat.* 1994, 166, paras 717–20.

28 *Cat.* 1994, 163, paras 703–4.

[29] Pope Paul VI, *Dei Verbum* (Dogmatic Constitution on Divine Revelation, 18 November 1965), 6; Pope Paul VI, *Gaudiam et Spes* (Pastoral Constitution (1) On the Church in the Modern World, 7 December 1965), 11.

[30] *Cat.* 1994, 252, para. 1098.

[31] Augustine, *Works*, 1991, II.2.7, 102, and IV.5.29, 174; Calvin, *Inst.*, I.13.14.

[32] Basil, *On the Spirit*, IX and XV, 43, 66; and the Catholic Church, *Cat.*, 163, paras 703–4.

[33] Colin E. Gunton, *The Triune Creator* (Edinburgh: Edinburgh University Press, 1998), 10.

[34] Canberra 1990–91 Consultation, 'Giver of Life – Sustain Your Creation!', W. Gramberg-Michaelson, 'Creation in Ecumenical Theology' in David G. Hallman (ed.), *Ecotheology: Voices from the South and North* (New York: Orbis, 1995), 100.

[35] Amos Yong, *Beyond the Impasse: Toward a Pneumatological Theology of Religions* (Grand Rapids: Baker Academic, 2003), 163f.

[36] Daniel W. Hardy, *God's Ways With the World: Thinking and Practising Christian Faith* (Edinburgh: T&T Clark, 1999), 17f.

[37] Hardy, *God's Ways*, 16f.

[38] Hardy, *God's Ways*, 17.

[39] 'The Chalcedonian Definition of the Faith' in J. Stevenson (ed.), *Creeds, Councils and Controversies: Documents Illustrating the History of the Church* A.D. *337–461* (London: SPCK, 1972), 337.

[40] The 'Tome' of Leo, 13 June 449, in Stevenson, *Creeds*, 315.

[41] W.H.C. Frend, *The Early Church: From the Beginnings to 461* (London: Hodder & Stoughton, 1965), 241.

[42] The discussion of this point is usually expressed through two terms that, for those inclined to use them, may simplify the idea. Jesus' human nature is *enhypostatos*, which means that it is 'in', or dependent on, the hypostasis of the divine nature. The human nature is therefore *anhypostatos*, which means that it has no hypostasis of its own without the divine hypostasis on which it is dependent. I hope that the explanation of this concept in simple English in the text is quite comprehensible without a more detailed explanation of the Greek terms. See Ferguson and Wright (eds), 'Hypostasis' in *New Dictionary*, 325; Karl Barth, *Unterricht in der christlichen Religion* (Zurich: Theologischer Verlag, 1990), *The Göttingen Dogmatics, Instruction in the Christian Religion*, tr. H. Reiffen and G.W. Bromiley (Grand Rapids: Eerdmans, 1991), vol. 1, 157.

[43] John Thompson, *Christ in Perspective in the Theology of Karl Barth* (Edinburgh: St Andrew Press, 1978), 84.

[44] Romans 8:3.

[45] Barth, *CD*, III/4, 42.

[46] Barth, *CD*, IV/2, 117.

7. Story and Meeting – Structure in Worship

[1] Austin Flannery, *Vatican Council II: The Conciliar and Post-Conciliar Documents* (Grand Rapids: Eerdmans, 1975), 6.

[2] Pope Pius X, *Inter Sollicitudies*, Motu Proprio of Pope St Pius X on Sacred Music, 22 November , 1903.

[3] Pope Paul VI, *Sacrosanctum Concilium*, 10.

[4] J. Sheppard, 'Worship' in Stanley M. Burgess and Eduard van der Maas (eds), *The New International Dictionary of Pentecostal and Charismatic Movements* (Grand Rapids: Zondervan, 2002), 1219.

[5] Walter J. Hollenweger, *Pentecostalism, Origins and Developments Worldwide* (Peabody, Mass.: Hendricksen, 1997), 270f.

[6] Daniel E. Albrecht, *Rites in the Spirit: A Ritual Approach to Pentecostal and Charismatic Spirituality* (Sheffield: Sheffield Academic Press, 1999), 179ff.

[7] Underhill, *Worship*, 312.

[8] 1 Kings 2:4; 8:25.

[9] 2 Chronicles 5:14.

[10] Pss. 50:2–3; 67:1; 118:26f.

[11] See also Pss. 46, 50, 81, 94:1, 108 and 132.

[12] 1 Timothy 2:1ff.; Ephesians 5:19; Colossians 3:16.

[13] 1 Corinthians 12:3.

[14] 1 Corinthians 14:17–18,26–33.

[15] 1 Timothy 4:13; Colossians 4:16; 1 Thessalonians 5:27.

[16] 2 Timothy 4:1–2.

[17] 2 Timothy 4:1.

[18] 1 Peter 2:9.

[19] Underhill, *Worship*, 86, 241.

[20] Alan Kreider, *Worship and Evangelism in Pre-Christendom* (Joint Liturgical Studies 32; Cambridge: Grove Books, 1995).

[21] Luther, *LW*, vol. 53, 25.

[22] John 4:23.

23 John 1:1; 21:22–3.
24 Revelations 4:11; 5:12.
25 Colossians 1:16.
26 Ephesians 1:22.
27 Josef A. Jungmann, *The Place of Christ in Liturgical Prayer*, tr. A. Peeler (London: Geoffrey Chapman, 1989), 127–71.
28 Torrance, *Worship*.

8. Putting the Frame in Place

1 M. Earey, 'This is the Word of the Lord: The Bible and Worship', *Anvil*, 19.2 (2002), 92f.
2 1 Timothy 4:13.
3 James H.S Steven, *Worship in the Spirit: Charismatic Worship in the Church of England* (Carlisle: Paternoster, 2002), 199.
4 C. Sunderland, 'Sinning against the earth?', *The Bible in Transmission* (Summer 2008), 16.
5 *CW*, 126f.
6 Daneel, *African Earthkeepers I*, 20.
7 Daneel, *African Earthkeepers I*, 94; Wapendama in Daneel, *African Earthkeepers II*, 359; Marinda in Daneel, *African Earthkeepers II*, 363f.
8 Philip Seddon, *Gospel and Sacrament: Reclaiming a Holistic Evangelical Spirituality* (Cambridge: Grove Books, 2004).
9 1 Timothy 2:1; Acts 3:23–30.
10 Ellis, *Gathering*, 119.

9. Creation Thinking in Worship

1 Claus Westermann in his Preface to *Blessing in the Bible and the Life of the Church* (Philadelphia: Fortress, 1978), xv.
2 Claus Westermann, *Elements of Old Testament Theology*, tr. D.W. Scott (Atlanta: John Knox, 1982), 112.
3 Genesis 1.22,28.
4 Westermann, *Elements*, 114.
5 Brueggemann in Westermann, *Blessing*, 1978, xi.
6 Westermann, *Elements*, 109.
7 Genesis 8:22.

[8] Roman Catholic Church, *Catechism of the Catholic Church* (London: Geoffrey Chapman, 1994), 248, para. 1083.

[9] Roman Catholic Church, *Sacrosanctum Concilium*, 61.

[10] R.T. Kendall, *Stand Up and be Counted* (London: Hodder & Stoughton, 1984), 77.

[11] Steven, *Worship*, 207.

[12] John Wimber and Kevin Springer, *Power Evangelism* (London: Hodder & Stoughton, 1985), 147; Tom Smail, Andrew Walker and Nigel Wright, *Charismatic Renewal: The Search for a Theology* (London: SPCK, 1993), 71f.

[13] Patrick Dixon, *Signs of Revival* (Eastbourne: Kingsway, 1994), 63.

[14] Wallace Boulton, *The Impact of Toronto* (Crowborough: Monarch, 1995), 111–15.

[15] P. Evokimov, 'La sacerduce universel des laïcs dans la tradition orientale' in L. Elchinger (ed.), *l'Eglise en dialogue* (Paris, 1962) 39f., quoted in Ware, *Inner Kingdom*, 68.

[16] *DL*, 49f.

[17] Hughes, 'Values and Religion', 20.

[18] Numbers 6:24–26.

[19] Genesis 48:15

[20] Paul Ricoeur, *Interpretation Theory: Discourse and the Surplus of Meaning* (Fort Worth: The Texas Christian University Press, 1976) 45–7, 52, 60, 67.

[21] Anthony Thiselton, *New Horizons in Hermeneutics* (London: HarperCollins, 1992), 357.

[22] Sally McFague, *Speaking in Parables: A Study in Metaphor and Theology* (London: SCM, 1975), xvi.

[23] Catherine Pickstock, *After Writing: On the Liturgical Consummation of Philosophy* (Oxford: Blackwell, 1998), 169f.

[24] In my service transcripts the category of metaphors represents about one fifth of the total number of lines where aspects of the doctrine of creation appear. In analysis of written liturgies a similar proportion occurs.

[25] Robert E. Webber, *Ancient-future Faith: Rethinking Evangelicalism for a Postmodern World* (Grand Rapids, Mich.: Baker Book House, 1999), 99f.; Nick Page, *And Now Let's Move into a Time of Nonsense: Why Worship Songs Are Failing the Church* (Milton Keynes: Authentic, 2004), 98–102.

[26] Paul Avis, *God and the Creative Imagination: Metaphor, Symbol and Myth in Religion and Theology* (London: Routledge, 1999), 51.

[27] This list is adapted from Leland Ryken, Jim Wilhoit and T. Longman (eds), *Dictionary of Biblical Imagery: An Encyclopaedic Exploration of the Images, Symbols, Motifs, Metaphors, Figures of Speech and Literary Patterns of the Bible* (Leicester: InterVarsity Press, 1998), xviii–xx.

[28] Caird, *Language and Imagery*, 154.

[29] Graham Kendrick, 'Shine Jesus Shine' (1987).

[30] Avis, 'God and the Creative Imagination', 85.

[31] Attributed to St Columba, in various collections of prayers.

[32] Andy Park, *Down the Mountain the River Flows* (1994).

[33] Thiselton, *Language, Liturgy and Meaning*, 26.

[34] Caird, *Language and Imagery*, 154.

[35] Ryken, Wilhoit and Longman, *Dictionary*, xvii.

[36] James Mays, ' "Maker of Heaven and Earth", Creation in the Psalms', in Brown and McBride, *God Who Creates*, 75.

[37] In researching this subject, I examined the presence of creation themes in the Psalms. Each psalm was placed in one of five categories according to the level of theological content on the subject of creation. Of the 150 psalms 42 are 'creation void'; 27 use creation metaphors to illustrate a subject other than creation; and 81 either deal with creation as a central theme, or include it in the subject matter, or indicate awareness of the creation dimension in some way.

10. Worshipping the Creator Every Week

[1] Elaine Ramshaw and Don S. Browning, *Ritual and Pastoral Care* (Philadelphia: Fortress, 1987).

[2] *Common Worship: Services and Prayers for the Church of England*, p. 104; *Common Worship: Times and Seasons*, p. 609.

[3] Staffordshire Seven, *Seasonal Worship*, and<www.farmingmatters .org.uk>.

[4] The Arthur Rank Centre, *Plough Sunday Worship Material, Rural Worship Resources* (2003) and other materials, see <www.arthurrank-centre.org.uk>.

[5] Church of England, *Common Worship: Times and Seasons* (London: Church House Publishing, 2006).

[6] Author unknown, *The Rushbearing in Grasmere* (Billingshurst: Weald Printers, undated).

[7] R. Christian, *Well-dressing in Derbyshire* (Derby: Derbyshire Countryside, 1998).

[8] Staffordshire Seven, *Seasonal Worship*, Introduction.

[9] The Church of Scotland Panel on Worship, *Book of Common Order of the Church of Scotland* (Edinburgh: St Andrew Press, 1996), 477, 483; the United Reformed Church, *Worship for the United Reformed Church* (London: the United Reformed Church, 2003), 15; the Baptist Union of Great Britain, Christopher Ellis and Myra Blyth (eds), *Gathering for Worship: Patterns and Prayers for the Community of Disciples* (Norwich: Canterbury Press, 2005), 398–400; the Methodist Church, *Our Common Ground* (Harvest Pack 2004), (London: Methodist Relief and Development Fund, 2004).

[10] Craig Millward, *Renewing Harvest: Celebrating God's Creation* (Edinburgh, Cambridge and Durham: Pentland Press, 2001), xviii.

[11] Mark Greene, 'Monday Morning Spirituality', *Bread for the Journey 2* (Farnham: CWR, 1988), 4.

[12] Designated by the United Nations as 5 June annually.

[13] World Day for Animals, 4 October annually.

[14] Ignatius, 'Epistle to the Magnesians', Ch. IX, *ANF*, 62.

[15] Justin Martyr, *Dialogue with Trypho*, Ch. XLI, *ANF*, 215.

[16] Irenaeus, *Against Heresies*, Book V, chap. XXIII, 2; chap. XXXIII, 1; chap. XXXVI, *ANF*, 551, 562, 566f.

[17] Moltmann, *God in Creation*, 6.

[18] Moltmann, *God in Creation*, 278–90.

[19] Wainwright, *Doxology*, 397; Millward, *Renewing*, 185.

[20] Douglas Davies, Charles Watkins and Michael Winter, *Church and Religion in Rural England* (Edinburgh: T&T Clark, 1991), 288.

[21] Sunderland, 'Sinning against the earth?' 16f.

[22] James F. White, *Protestant Worship: Traditions in Transition* (Louisville: Westminster John Knox, 1989), 60.